W9-CLW-979

Twayne's United States Authors Series

Sylvia E. Bowman, *Editor*

INDIANA UNIVERSITY

Albion W. Tourgée

ALBION W. TOURGÉE

---

by Theodore L. Gross
The City College of New York

 39

CARNEGIE LIBRARY
LIVINGSTONE COLLEGE
SALISBURY, N. C. 28144

Twayne Publishers, Inc.   ::   New York

Copyright © 1963 by Twayne Publishers, Inc.

Library of Congress Catalog Card Number: 63-10956

MANUFACTURED IN THE UNITED STATES OF AMERICA BY
UNITED PRINTING SERVICES, INC.
NEW HAVEN, CONN.

13,49
645 g
73150

TO THE MEMORY OF MY FATHER

Preface

IN RECONCILING DIFFERENCES between the North and South, the writers of Reconstruction played an important role. They helped to ease social and political conflicts during Reconstruction and, in the 1880's and 1890's, they toned down sectional hostility by creating an enormous body of palliative fiction that was widely popular. Any chronicle of the restitution of a nationalism free from sectional animosity must include the contributions of such authors as Joel Chandler Harris, Thomas Nelson Page, Paul Hamilton Hayne, Constance Fenimore Woolson, and John W. De Forest. For it was these authors (whose works were emulated by a legion of more obscure, even subliterary writers) who sponsored an amicable restoration of the Union.

Reconstruction authors, in helping to restore national harmony, offered superficial descriptions of the post-bellum period; for they were obviously propagandists for peace, and their works were not artistically compelling. Few had experienced the period as adults, while none—with the significant exception of Albion W. Tourgée—reported the Reconstruction era from the point of view of a Radical Republican. In the fiction of Southern local colorists, the carpetbagger is the villain and the scalawag is his conspiratorial partner; in the fiction of Northern authors the same stereotypes are drawn, and sympathy is extended toward the displaced Southern gentry.

Tourgée occupies a unique position among the writers of Reconstruction literature. He was the only Northerner who wrote extensively about the period; the only writer who had lived in the South during the Reconstruction era; and, of greater importance, he was the only author who was an active politician in the carpetbagger regime. His best work has a personal and authoritative spirit that humanizes Reconstruction and forces the reader to share the suffering of all men—Southern as well as Northern—in this tragic era.

Tourgée's fiction is a rationalization of the Radical Republican performance during Reconstruction; as such, it is as biased and erroneous as the report of Southern authors like Harris, Page, and Thomas Dixon. Certain historical facts are disregarded in Tourgée's version of Reconstruction, just as similar facts are too prominent in the novels of Southern writers. Tourgée ignores the misdemeanors of Negroes; Southerners exaggerate their crimes. Tourgée censures the Southern gentleman as a white supremacist who is unwilling to provide the Negro political and civil equality; Southern authors depict the gentleman as a man defending a civilization which has been invaded by corrupt, venal, and opportunistic carpetbaggers. In Tourgée's works, the Republican is the humanitarian, the selfless reformer interested in providing justice for the Negro and in helping to reconstruct the backward South; in the fiction of Southerners he is indifferent to the best interests of the South—the good work attempted by many Republicans is almost totally ignored.

The facts indicate that Tourgée's report of Reconstruction was truer of Tourgée himself than of other Radical Republicans in North Carolina. To a great extent he was a humanitarian, a man who interpreted political problems in moral terms, who felt the need to serve some "noble cause"; and, unlike other Northern travelers in the South, he slowly grew to appreciate and understand the Southern point of view. His attempt to help reconstruct the South resulted in political and social failure, and his writings are a measurement of that failure—of what he came to regard as "a fool's errand." Since Tourgée's important novels are inextricably related to his political and social activities, his experiences in North Carolina are examined closely in the following study; against this background his fictional description of Reconstruction is measured as the record—and eventual vindication—of a political attitude which was uniformly attacked by late nineteenth-century writers.

In 1947, George J. Becker was able to state that "Albion W. Tourgée is perhaps the most neglected figure in American literature. Nothing of importance has been written about him since Roy F. Dibble's biography twenty-five years ago. . . . Yet Tourgée, who preceded nearly all of them [post-Civil War authors], whose work is on a far larger scale than that of any other social critic before 1890, and whose novel A Fool's Errand enjoyed a phenomenal popularity, is today largely unknown."[1] Becker's observation is no longer completely true, for several estimates have appeared in the past decade. Nevertheless, there is still no full-length examination of Tourgée as a Reconstruction author. This study is an attempt to acquaint the student of American literature with a novelist who has been too long neglected; it is an attempt to restore Tourgée to his proper role as a significant interpreter and remarkably powerful reporter of the Reconstruction era. Of all the authors of Reconstruction fiction, Tourgée was most directly aware of the politics of the post-bellum South. His writings, unlike those of Page, Harris, and Thomas Dixon, are not a recollection; they are an intimate, contemporaneous, cogently rendered account of Reconstruction.

In the preparation of this book, I have incurred many debts of gratitude. Mr. Rodney Nixon granted me access to the Tourgée collection at the Chatauqua County Historical Museum, Westfield, New York, when the museum was officially closed. The manuscripts, letters, and other materials in this collection are described in the bibliography.

Professor David Donald read an earlier draft of the manuscript and advised me on historical matters. Professors Richard Chase, Lewis Leary, Eleanor Tilton, and Sylvia Bowman offered me constant encouragement, for which I am grateful, and helped to improve the writing and general organization of the book. My greatest debt of all is to my wife Selma, who read more drafts of this study than I dare to remember; her invaluable criticism has improved the manuscript at every stage of its development.

THEODORE L. GROSS

The City College of New York
New York City
July, 1962

Contents

Chronology

1838   On May 2, Albion W. Tourgée was born on a farm in Williamsfield, Ashtabula County, Ohio, the son of Valentine and Louisa Tourgée.

1854   Tourgée attended the Kingsville Academy in Kingsville, Ohio.

1859   Tourgée entered the University of Rochester, received the sophomore rating, and stayed there until January, 1861, when he was compelled to leave because of lack of financial resources.

1861   In January, he became associate principal of a school at Wilson, Niagara County, New York. In April he enlisted in the 27th New York Volunteers and in July received a wound in his spine.

1862   In June, he was granted the bachelor's degree from the University of Rochester. In July, he went to Columbus and received a commission as first lieutenant in Company G of the 105th Ohio Volunteers.

1863   On May 14, Tourgée was married at Columbus, Ohio.

1864   On January 1, he withdrew from the army.

1865   On October 14, he and his wife moved to Greensboro, North Carolina.

1866   In September he was a delegate to the Loyalist convention held at Philadelphia.

1867   Beginning January 3, 1867, Tourgée edited a Republican newspaper in Greensboro, *The Union Register*. But it failed by June 14, and it was transferred to Raleigh under a different management.

1868   On March 21, he was elected a judge of the Superior Court, Seventh Judicial District of North Carolina. He began his duties August, 1868, and served for six years. He was appointed one of the three commissioners for a term of three years to codify the laws of the state. Together with Victor C. Barringer and Will B. Rodman, he published *The Code of Civil Procedure to Special Pleadings.*

1874 *'Toinette: a Novel,* published under the nom de plume "Henry Churton"; reappeared as *A Royal Gentleman* (1881).

1876 Tourgée was appointed Pension Agent at Raleigh by President Grant.

1879 Tourgée left North Carolina on September 2. *Figs and Thistles,* published on October 4; *A Fool's Errand,* November 15.

1880 *The Invisible Empire,* published with *A Fool's Errand,* May 22; *Bricks Without Straw* (several reprints on unknown dates).

1881 *A Royal Gentleman* published (*'Toinette* renamed). In October a dramatization of *A Fool's Errand* appeared in Philadelphia. This was written in collaboration with Steele McKaye. It failed.

1882 *John Eax and Mamelon* published. *Our Continent,* begun under Tourgée's editorship on February 15, continued until August 20, 1884.

1883 *Hot Plowshares* was serialized in *Our Continent* from July, 1882–May, 1883.

1884 *An Appeal to Caesar* published, a sociological tract written in fulfillment of a promise made to President Garfield.

1885 "A Man of Destiny" written for the *Daily Inter Ocean* and published weekly from December, 1884–March, 1885; "Letters to a Mugwump," in *Daily Inter Ocean* from September–November; "The Veteran and His Pipe," in *Inter Ocean,* April–September.

1886 "A Child of Luck" published in *Inter Ocean,* March–July.

1887 *Black Ice* published in May. *Button's Inn* published.

1888 *Eighty-Nine, or The Grand Master's Story* published in April under the nom de plume of Edgar Henry. *Letters to a King* published. "A Bystander's Notes" published

May 5, 1888–January, 1895; August, 1897–September, 1898, in the *Inter Ocean.*

1889 *With Gauge and Swallow, Attorneys* serialized in *Lippincott's Monthly Magazine,* December, 1887–August, 1889.

1890 *Pactolus Prime* published in March; *Murvale Eastman,* in November.

1891 In July, Tourgée published "John Workman's Notions" in the *Inter Ocean.*

1892 *A Son of Old Harry.*

1893 *Out of the Sunset Sea.*

1894 *An Outing with the Queen of Hearts.* From January to April, "A Man of Destiny" appeared weekly in the *Inter Ocean.*

1895 In the spring, Tourgée edited *The Basis: A Journal of Citizenship* whose mission was "The Basis of Public Peace, Personal Security, Equal Rights, Justice to All, Good Laws, Good Government, National Prosperity, Improved Conditions, AND OF A BETTER WORLD TOMORROW." The newspaper failed because of insufficient funds in April, 1896.

1896 *The War of Standards* published: a study in "coin and credit versus coin without credit." *The Mortgage of the Hip-Roof House* published.

1897 On May 6, Tourgée was appointed consul to Bordeaux, France. On July 3, he and his family sailed for France.

1898 *The Man Who Outlived Himself* published.

1901 "The Summerdale Brabble" appeared in *The National Tribune,* March–April.

1905 On May 21, Tourgée died in Bordeaux.

CHAPTER 1

The Genesis of Folly

TOURGÉE'S early life prepared him, religiously and intellectually, for his role as the interpreter of the Negro's dilemmas in the post-bellum South. Born on a farm in Ashtabula, Ohio, on May 2, 1838, he was brought up by a stepmother and a strict Methodist father, Valentine Tourgée, who instilled in his son two fundamental characteristics which served him well in later life: a religious awareness and a fondness for debate. Valentine Tourgée was a stern moralist who had a reputation for delivering "enormously long supplications in the weekly prayer meetings" which could "be heard far beyond the wall of the church itself." With a love of argument, father and son "would, in the midst of a tempestuous debate, seat themselves at the table, when, of course, it was necessary to pause briefly for the saying of grace; and once this perfunctory task had been performed as speedily as possible, the verbal combat would be renewed with greater violence than ever."[1]

The father was intellectually inclined, but his library included only religious works such as the Bible, Goodrich's *Universal History,* a general *History of the United States, Pilgrim's Progress,* Bacon's *Essays, Paradise Lost, Night Thoughts,* and D'Aubigne's *History of the Reformation;* he compelled his son to memorize parts of these volumes "for his soul's good and incidentally as a punishment for childish offences." Valentine Tourgée had once intended to follow a profession, "but financial loss, and more particularly a strong religious awakening" had turned his mind from these pursuits "and also from the making of verse in which he had occasionally indulged." He burned the fiction in his library and insisted that his son read only literature of an "inspiring and edifying" nature.[2]

Tourgée rebelled against this rigid upbringing—at one point

in his adolescence he left his home and escaped for a two-year period to a sympathetic Winegar uncle in Lee, Massachusetts— but some of his later characteristics indicate the powerful influence of his father. There is a dominating note of idealism in all of his work, and his public acts are almost always predicated on some moral assumption; this religious strain is combined with an unyielding independence and stubbornness which he also inherited from his father.

It was not until the younger Tourgée attended the Kingsville Academy in Kingsville, Ohio, in 1854 that he was able to read those works—all the novels of Scott and Cooper, for example— which later determined his notion of what a novel ought to be. At this time he began to write essays and poetry, and there remains among his manuscripts a notebook entitled "Bits of Sense and Nonsense," which contains youthful poems written in the style of Byron. But Tourgée had no serious intention of becoming an author during his academy days; and, when he was graduated from the Kingsville Academy in 1859, he had already determined to "follow the legal profession."[3]

Entering the University of Rochester in the autumn of 1859, Tourgée studied only those subjects which interested him. He read poetry voraciously; he studied "Shakespeare . . . and all the pre-Shakespearean dramatists"; he excelled in logic and languages and took part in many debates; but "mathematics was his special aversion." Tourgée, who had little interest in politics in 1859 and the early part of 1860, believed that "the Union might be dissolved and the whole Creation go to smash without my knowing anything about it unless some fierce Southern fire-eaters should see fit to honor me with a rope." He confessed that he knew "absolutely nothing about Politics," had no "time to read Politics," and didn't "care a copper which [section] whips."[4] But as hostilities increased between North and South, Tourgée became interested in political affairs, sympathizing immediately with the Republican party. By October, 1860, he and other students organized the "Rochester Wide Awake Club," a group devoted to the Republican cause, and Tourgée "was elected captain"; but the president of the college, Martin B. Anderson, objected to any "popular agitation of the delicate and dangerous questions" before the nation, and Tourgée's club was disbanded.[5]

Tourgée left the University of Rochester in January, 1861.

because of lack of funds; in April he enlisted in the 27th New York Volunteers. He fought in the first battle of Bull Run on July 4, 1861, where he was wounded in the spine, an injury which was to cause him lifelong pain. Granted an honorable discharge, he was sent to his home in Ashtabula, Ohio. At this time he showed his first professional interest in law; from August, 1861, to July, 1862, he "read Blackstone every day" and studied law at the office of Sherman and Farmer, Ashtabula, Ohio.[6]

But Tourgée could not remain at home for long while the country was at war, and by July, 1862, he was well enough to re-enter the army. He received a commission as first lieutenant in Company G of the 105th Ohio Volunteers. The Volunteers fought in the campaign against the Confederates at Tullahoma in June, 1862, and were involved in the battles of Chickamauga, Chattanooga, Lookout Mountain, and Missionary Ridge.[7] In September, 1862, Tourgée's concern for the Negro first became evident; he was "put under arrest . . . for refusing to surrender a colored man who had saved [his] company."[8] A year later he applied for a transfer to a Negro regiment, certain that "this was the best place for men who serve the country best."[9] The transfer was never granted, however, and Tourgée remained with the Ohio Volunteers until he was discharged from the army on January 1, 1864.

Tourgée's unrestrained sympathy for the Negro—his tireless desire to grant the Negro equal rights—persisted throughout his life and was responsible for the hostility of many Southerners. When Tourgée moved to the South in 1865, he brought with him just those attitudes which Southerners hated most: a belief that the South had to be "Americanized" and a desire to raise the Negro to immediate equality. Tourgée was not a politician when he came to North Carolina, but he was prepared to be one; he was not a leader of the Negroes, yet he championed their rights, sought their support, and soon established himself as one of their firmest advocates. In only a few years, he was being attacked by a leading Southerner as the most *"detestable character"* in the state.[10]

Politically and economically this period from 1865 to 1879 was for Tourgée a failure; it proved to be more frustrating than fruitful. Tourgée himself later referred to it as the time of his foolish errand. In terms of his career as a writer and journalist, however, he could not have made a wiser choice of a place to live; for he discovered in the South a subject well suited to his independent, aggressive temperament. His experiences there were by far the most important of his entire life; and, since they form the basis of his finest fiction, we will examine them in some detail.

I   A Carpetbagger in the South

In June, 1865, Tourgée wrote a long letter to the provisional governor of North Carolina, William W. Holden, requesting information for one "desirous of moving to the Old North State." A Northern veteran of the Civil War who was just beginning his career in law, Tourgée inquired about the economic and social conditions of the South; he wondered whether a Union man would be welcomed by his former enemy. Holden assured him that there was "nothing in the feeling of the loyal people of this state which would make it unpleasant for northern labor to come into our midst."[11] These remarks were deceptive, for in speaking of "loyal people" Holden was referring to those Unionists who had belonged to the peace movement during the war and who now formed the Union party; had Holden said "the Republicans of the state," his letter would have been less misleading. He did not indicate the great hostility a Radical Republican would encounter in North Carolina; and Tourgée assumed, as he wrote later, that "manufactures [would] spring up, immigration [would] pour in, and it [would] be just the pleasantest part of the country."[12] In July, 1865, Tourgée left his home in Ashtabula, Ohio, and traveled throughout North Carolina seeking a home. He finally selected Greensboro because of the opportunity to engage in a nursery business as well as in his regular profession of lawyer.[13]

Tourgée's ignorance of Southern life in 1865 was typical of that of the victorious Northerner; "it was a surprise almost," he remarked years later, "to hear the same language spoken."[14] He had no real understanding of the aristocratic tradition, the deep-rooted pride, the hardened independence, that most travelers of the late 1860's attributed to the Southerner; and, as was true of his fellow Northerners, his immediate reaction to the South was antagonistic.

Like John T. Trowbridge and Sidney Andrews, journalists who offered Northerners their first post-bellum descriptions of Southern life, Tourgée viewed the South as barbarous, as requiring the civilizing influence of the North. Trowbridge claimed that there existed great danger "of *unarmed* rebellion, of continued sectional strife, stirred up by Southern politicians" who "commanded the sympathies of the Southern people,"[15] while Andrews believed that it would "not be safe to admit" Southern representatives "to their seats at present. Some of them ought never to be admitted. They have no business in a congress of the United States, for they are either of bitterly rebellious spirit or are encased in the poisonous bigotries of State supremacy."[16] Tourgée was in general agreement with this opinion of the South when he first came to North Carolina, and by 1866 it became obvious that he was even more radical than Trowbridge, Andrews, and most of the Republicans in North Carolina.

The impetuous Tourgée, eager to rise both politically and financially, soon established himself as one of the most controversial figures ever to live in North Carolina—a carpetbag-lawyer who intended to help the freedmen obtain justice in the South. The conditions of the South and the debasement that the Negro suffered appalled him. One-third of the Southern people and seventy-two per cent of the Negroes were illiterate, and the whites and freedmen were more estranged than ever before. Some Southerners were bitter, implacable men who felt, as one South Carolinian noted, that the Yankees had left them but "one inestimable privilege—to hate 'em."[17] Yet most Southerners were sick of battle and eager to rebuild their homes; "the war spirit is gone, and no fury can re-enliven it,"[18] a Northern observer recorded. The common Southern feeling was that they had been thoroughly whipped, and they now wanted Northerners to cease reproaching them.[19]

But Tourgée, like many Radicals, felt himself on an "errand" of enlightenment; he intended to help establish racial equality in the "poor, misguided and mismanaged South," to "loose" Southerners "from the slough of ignorance and prejudice." Tourgée realized "that the advocacy of Union principles; or, if you prefer the word, radical principles, is anything but a popular movement in any part of the South," but it was what he had "enlisted for."[20] He considered himself an "unfaltering champion of true and absolute Republicanism," and those "hundreds of North Carolinians" who were his supporters were to be "regarded as the forlorn hope of true Republicanism in the state."[21] Consequently, he was confronted with the immediate resistance of the majority of Southern whites who did not seek advice from intruding carpetbaggers.

The Southerners' strong feeling of hostility was aggravated by the Radicals themselves. They were impetuous and selfish in many of their aims, and Southerners were convinced, often with good reason, that the Republicans manipulated the Negro's vote.[22] Tourgée, who had originally migrated to the South for the purpose of restoring his health, became involved in Reconstruction politics shortly after his arrival in Greensboro. He not only opposed the Conservatives in newspaper writings and speeches but also criticized many Southern Republicans whose politics, he felt, were neither radical nor consistent enough. These Republicans—native North Carolinians like W. W. Holden, Thomas Settle, Robert P. Dick, James H. Harris, William P. Bynum, William B. Rodman, and Edwin G. Reade—had been members of the peace movement during the war and had advocated at that time an end to hostilities and a championing of the Union.[23]

Tourgée opposed these Southern Republicans because they had originally agreed to secession and had permitted themselves to be controlled by Confederates. He thought in April, 1866, that the passive secessionists were tacitly loyal "to certain men who [had] led them by the nose from infancy to manhood, and these men [were] the leaders of the late rebellion."[24] The leader of the Southern Republicans, W. W. Holden, was appointed provisional governor by President Johnson in 1865; and with his supporters he formed a political group known as the Union party. On racial matters, Holden followed a moderate course of action. He favored Negro rights, but he was afraid of strong Conservative opposition and in August of 1866 declared himself against Negro suffrage; by December, however, he "promoted negro suffrage as violently as he opposed it in the past" and advocated a reorganization on the basis of "loyal white and black suffrage."[25] Holden felt that "latter-day war men" should be proscribed and that "all male citizens of North Carolina who could read or write, or who owned real estate to the value of one hundred dollars, could vote. No person who formerly had the right to vote could be disqualified."[26] During the last few months of 1866, Holden's Union party supported the passage of the Fourteenth Amendment, but Conservatives violently denounced the bill. Tourgée thought that Southerners were wise not to destroy themselves politically by ratifying the amendment; in later years he termed it as "a makeshift, inspired by fright at what had been done, and a desire to avoid what must be done."[27]

Naturally Tourgée objected to the Conservative political position; but he also opposed the moderation of the Holdenites. On January 3, 1867, he began to edit *The Union Register*, a newspaper that advocated the most radical measures. "*The act of rebellion disfranchised all who participated in it voluntarily,*" he wrote in the first issue and went on to say that only "loyal constituents" should be tolerated.[28] Such a proposal, which would have prevented many Republicans from holding political office, was attacked by members of Holden's Union party. Tourgée refused to recognize that Southern Republicans had to submit to the dominance of the Conservatives during the war and that many of them now realized the difficulties involved in urging immediate and complete suffrage for the Negro. Holden tried to pacify Tourgée by paying tribute to "our friends of the *Union Register*" and by saying that Tourgée "was very popular with the Unionists and will wield a strong influence in the Western portion of this state."[29]

But Tourgée would not be mollified. He attacked the moderate position of the Union party, claiming that he was "against rebel hope, rebel ambition, and Confederate resurrection"[30] and that he was in favor of making the Southern states territories until the completion of Reconstruction.[31] Moreover, he warned the Negro of Holden's Union party, writing in April, 1867, that "To the real, life-long friend of the colored people, to the believers in equality, and the life-long abolitionist, this does not *all* bode good"; he admonished Negroes to "shrink from their [Holdenites'] caress."[32]

Tourgée was criticized by Southern Unionists for splitting the Republican party in North Carolina. Certainly he was naïve in using a wartime allegiance to the Confederacy as a test for postwar loyalty to the Union. He revived the dead issues of secession and war, fearful that the Union party would control and misdirect the Negro and Unionist voters; but he underestimated the political solidarity of Union party members and their support of both Unionism and reform. As one moderate Republican observed, Republican leaders like W. W. Holden, R. P. Dick, Thomas Settle, "and others in this state have stood up and stood out against them [the Conservatives] in this state

in the face of heavy odds. It was *worth something* to stand out
against the party in this state during the war. It was different
in the North. It was—*easier than any other* to be a Union man
there. Opposing and endeavoring to thwart the secessionists here
was about all we *could* do.[33] In later years most of the
Holdenites became the most faithful and prominent members
of the Republican party, and Tourgée himself admired them.

II *The Radical Politician*

On June 14, 1867, Tourgée's newspaper *The Union Register*
expired because of lack of funds, and the impact of his hostility
was reduced. Nevertheless, he continued as an outspoken member of the Radical Republicans. Most of these extreme Republicans—men like Wilson Carey, Harmon Unthank, Wyatt Outlaw,
J. W. Stephens, W. A. Allbright, G. W. Welker, and David
Hodgin—had little education, wealth, or political experience.
Consequently, Tourgée, with his education, was able to assert
himself as a leader of this faction. In 1866 he helped to organize
the Loyal Reconstruction League "in Guildford, Alamance, and
the adjoining counties,"[34] and it was his work with this pro-
Negro group that had originally aroused the ire of North
Carolinians.

When W. W. Holden was proposed as "Grand President of the
ULA [Union League of America] for the State of North Carolina"
in March of 1867, Tourgée objected, feeling that Holden was
untrustworthy and not Unionist enough. Tourgée declined to
unite his local group with the Union League of America; but the
national chief, J. M. Edmunds, in a letter dated March 3, 1867,
informed him that such opposition was not politically advisable:
"We cannot stand upon personal objections in this contest and
if we attempt it, we shall find few men to whom none will
object, and possibly very few who would be less objectionable
than Gov Holden."[35]

Tourgée, who was associated with only a small group of
extreme Unionists, was not powerful enough to oppose Holden,
or the Republican leaders in Washington; and in April, 1867,
he pledged the loyalty of his supporters and himself. Holden
was appointed "Grand President of ULA for State of North
Carolina" and Tourgée a "Deputy of the Grand Council of the

Order for the State of North Carolina."[36] Tourgée's close
association with the Union League proved to be profitable when
he came to trace the history of the organization in *A Fool's
Errand* (1879), although his fictional treatment of Reconstruction presents his hero, modeled on himself, as less personally
and politically involved with the League.

Tourgée was in fact one of the most active and popular speech
makers at League meetings, and the major message of all his
speeches was that the freedman's interests were irreconcilably
opposed to those of the Southern whites. At one meeting in
May, 1867, he announced his support of free public schools,
repeated his belief in the equality of all men, and endorsed
the Reconstruction Acts.[37] Often urged by other Radicals to
speak before a *"great mass* meeting," he was assured by them
that he was able to "do more good than anybody else."[38] Seem-
ingly he cared little for his own person, and he made such
vituperative attacks on national figures that one Southerner—
J. M. McCorkle, a respected lawyer of Salisbury and a supporter
of W. W. Holden—recalled years later that Tourgée "let fly a
speech at Andrew Johnson which, I reckon, made him the most
hated man in all that community. He said he was worse than
Catiline; that he was no improvement on Jefferson Davis, etc.
While we listened in speechless disgust, I couldn't help admiring
the persistence and pluck of the little devil."[39]

But Tourgée antagonized the people of North Carolina to an
even greater degree when he told Northerners of the mistreatment
of Negroes and of Union men in his adopted state. At the
Loyalist Convention, held at Philadelphia in September, 1866,
he spread scurrilous, unsubstantiated rumors regarding political
affairs in Guilford County and in the entire state. He was the
most prominent delegate from North Carolina and was particularly effective in the ensuing debate dealing with Negro
suffrage. Naturally he endorsed the vote for the Negro, claiming
that it was necessary to protect not only the freedman but the
Union as well. At this time he said that he was the representative
of two thousand Union men in North Carolina and claimed to
be their mouthpiece; these men, he reported, "demanded two
conditions:— 1st. The disfranchisement of all traitors. 2nd. The
enfranchisement of all loyal men." He went on to affirm that
no loyal man was safe in North Carolina and that "he had been

lately informed 'by a Quaker' that the bodies of fifteen negroes had been dragged out of one pond in Guilford County." He also stated that "1,200 Union soldiers, who had settled in the State, had been forced to sacrifice their property and leave the State to save their lives."[40] But this was an obvious lie, for "at that time the military authorities were making close investigations, and no one else heard of such an incident."[41] Tourgée also asserted that he knew of one hundred of the

> loyal men who were threatened with death if they wore the blue, [and who were] now wearing the grey. . . . Several hundred loyal men had petitioned President Johnson for redress from the rebel depredations, and the petition was referred back to the disloyal Governor of that State, and came back to the authorities of their own town. I know the intents, purposes, and feelings of those men, what they are pledged to, and their necessities. I want to ask now, not politicians or Congress, but the loyal men of the North, through their press and their pulpits to give us help ere we die. Is there no rescue for us? Shall we save the Union there? Shall we continue the rebels in power, in office, on the bench, and the Union men in the dungeon?[42]

Jonathan Worth, who had been elected governor in November, 1865, believed Tourgée's speech "to be a tissue of lies from beginning to end" and knew that his statement referring to the petition was untrue; Worth had never received any petition from Tourgée.[43] In other speeches delivered in Pennsylvania, Tourgée further condemned the "uncompromising Rebels" of North Carolina. "The enemy whom we thought we had routed has merely executed a flank movement," he claimed. In the "spirit of the South today" a "Reconstructionist [is] considered a fool"; Southerners "hate Yankees" and "kill Negroes." Southern Unionists like himself, he maintained, "are a political minority," suffering "legal disabilities and persecutions." Tourgée urged as the only possible solutions the "disfranchisement of Rebels" and the "enfranchisement of Black Unionists," solutions which had to be put into effect immediately.[44]

Upon his return to Greensboro, Tourgée discovered that because of his unsubstantiated statements at the Philadelphia convention his life was in constant danger. North Carolinians were convinced of his unscrupulous behavior as a politician, and many of them sent threatening letters to him and his wife:

Greensboro, Sept., 1866

A. W. Tourgée

It is about time that your lying tong [*sic*] was stopped—and if you ever show your ugly face in Guilford County again I will take care with some of my friends that you find the bottom of that niger [*sic*] pond you have been talking so much about—I warn you never to show yourself in this county again.

On the 24th of the same month another local citizen demanded Tourgée's immediate departure from the South:

. . . You knew that what you said in that convention was fake. You knew that 1200 ex-Federal soldiers had not been driven from the state. You knew that 15 dead negroes had not been taken from 1 pond. You knew that Southern Loyalists and negroes are safe here provided that they behave themselves. You were suffered to insult us before you went to the convention but you will not be suffered to come back and insult us. Your stay in N. C. had better be short if you expect to breathe the vital air.[45]

Letters of a slightly more friendly nature were sent to Tourgée's wife, advising her to urge her husband to be more prudent. "Even ladies (and I blush to write it) are saying that he ought to be served to a suit of tar and feathers," one person, evidently a woman, wrote. "I was born in the South and I know the character of the Southern people. There is a class of ignorant people which has always been under the influence and designing of evil leaders and has always done their miserable work."[46] Tourgée paid little attention to these threats and friendly admonitions, and he continued his sincere and tireless devotion toward the Negro.

The Radicals and the members of Holden's Union party in North Carolina promoted agitation whenever possible. Tourgée himself delivered many speeches in Pennsylvania and later in North Carolina. His letters of 1866 read like the documents of a young man who sees himself as one of the leaders of a great movement in history: "I have to speak almost every day and would not stop if I could," he wrote his wife on September 16. "I know I am doing good for the great cause."[47]

In the following year, the First Reconstruction Act, sponsored by the Radical Republicans, was put into operation. The Northern attitude toward the South was defined now, and the citizens in general knew of the national policy that had been established. The basic act of March 2, 1867, "consisted of two distinct parts: five of its six sections provided for establishment of a rigorous and comprehensive military government throughout the ten states not yet restored to the Union; while the remaining section, the fifth, declared that the restoration of the states should be effected only after reorganization, on the basis of general negro enfranchisement and limited rebel disfranchisement."[48]

Holden and his Union party were satisfied with this and subsequent Reconstruction Acts; some members of his party were even enthusiastic.[49] Tourgée, however, felt that there was not enough federal control of the states and that those Republicans in North Carolina who were to enforce the measures suffered, as he said in *Bricks Without Straw* (1880), from "ignorance and poverty," as opposed to Conservatives who had "intelligence, wealth and pride."[50] The federal government had compelled the South to accept emancipation; similarly, Tourgée maintained, it should have forced the South to accept the civil and political equality of the Negro. Tourgée was not opposed to the Reconstruction Acts in principle; he felt that practically they would not succeed so long as any control was left in the hands of the states. He objected to all those "who accept the terms on which the nation gave re-established and greatly-increased power to the states of the South."[51]

Confronted with a choice between the Conservatives and the Republicans, Tourgée naturally associated himself with the latter political group. Nevertheless, he continued to distrust Holden; he felt himself, as a consistent Unionist, to be entitled to take a leading role in the new federal program and resented the position of leadership that Holden and his Union party assumed. Although he continued to criticize Holden privately—and only once openly—from June, 1867, until his departure from the South, Tourgée was Holden's political ally. As a Republican, he really had no choice at all; Holden was the leader of the Republicans, and Tourgée knew that, if he wanted a political life in North Carolina, he had to ally himself with Holden.

United now with the dominant group of Republicans in the state, Tourgée became an earnest advocate of many reform measures. He was active at the North Carolina State Convention held in Raleigh in 1868, where "he not only acted as chief marshal at the Raleigh meeting, but served on the Republican state executive committee."[52] He was probably the most influential man in the proceedings of the convention,[53] largely because "the great body of the membership had no qualification for the duty they had undertaken [the framing of a state constitution]. Under these circumstances the work was naturally performed by a few leaders," among whom was Tourgée.[54] The constitution, of which Tourgée was one of the chief framers, was patterned after those of Ohio and progressive Northern states—states from which those Radical leaders had emigrated.

Years later, Tourgée wrote to his daughter that "the fear of starvation and shame led me to fight for a place as a member of the Constitutional Convention of 1868. I found myself the strongest man in it."[55] Yet he was not strong enough to put through many of his proposals and reform measures. He was an earnest advocate of repudiating the entire state debt, feeling that the new state of North Carolina, which the members at the Convention were constructing, was under no obligation to pay the debts of the old and that it would be disastrous to do so. He claimed that "he would be a fool who would emigrate to North Carolina if the new State is to be saddled with the debts of the old."[56] But his view was not shared by the majority of those present, and the section of the Bill of Rights which guaranteed the public debt of the state was adopted. A fellow carpetbagger, Joseph C. Abbott, called Tourgée's doctrine infamous; and even three Negro delegates voiced their horror at his proposal.

Some of the significant changes in the constitution which Tourgée advocated were, as a recent historian has noted, "modern, progressive, liberal and democratic."[57] They included the abolition of slavery; provision for universal suffrage, white and Negro; the elimination of all property and religious qualifications for voting and office-holding (except the disbarment of atheists from public office); popular election of state and county officials; abolition of the county court system and the adoption of the township county commission form of local government; and provisions for a Board of Charities and Public Welfare and for "a general and uniform system of Public Schools" to be open "for at least four months in every year."[58] "The new constitution wrought many changes in ideas of government," wrote a Justice of the Supreme Court of North Carolina in 1944, "but it was well grounded in the American concept of representative government, liberal and progressive, and after 76 years remains practically unchanged, either in form or substance. Though the conservative forces soon regained political control of the state and have retained their power almost continuous to this time, the constitution of 1868 still stands as the basic law of the commonwealth."[59]

III *The Prominent Judge*

At the 1868 convention Tourgée had been hardly aware "that he was committing an enormity" against the Southern people by advocating so many reforms; but, as he himself remarked later, "from that day he became an outlaw in the land where he had hoped to have made a home, and which he desired faithfully to serve."[60] During the next eleven years of residence in North Carolina he continued to resist the Southern suppression of the Negro in all political areas and thus encouraged the active opposition of such public officials as Jonathan Worth, governor of North Carolina until 1868. No one attacked Tourgée more than he, and his correspondence bristles with stinging remarks about the incorrigible Radical, the man "of most 'detestable character' in this state. . . ."[61] Worth, unsparing in his criticism of Tourgée, characterized him as "the meanest Yankee who ever settled among us."[62] In offering his reason for objecting to Tourgée as a judge, Worth remarked: "I am sure I have heard more than 100 men speak of Tourgée as a man of 'most contemptible character' and I never heard one speak well of him."[63]

Worth had been especially provoked by the speech Tourgée had delivered at the Loyalist Convention in Philadelphia in September, 1866, which denounced Southern atrocities against the Negro. In the early part of 1867, when the judge of the Superior Court, Seventh Judicial District, resigned, Tourgée was suggested as his replacement, and "he would have been appointed but for the opposition of Governor Worth."[64] Worth was certain of "the utter disgust [that] all respectable people of this state would feel at putting on our bench of judges such a wretch as Tourgée who stinks in the nostrils of all men of honor";[65] but his opposition to Tourgée was only temporarily effective, for Tourgée accepted the nomination for the office of judge on March 21, 1868, and in the April elections he won the position by a majority of more than twenty-five thousand votes.[66]

Tourgée's letter accepting the nomination is of particular interest, for it contains one of the clearest statements of his beliefs regarding the office of judge:

In accepting the nomination I speak as a Republican. . . . For this party therefore I am ready and willing at all times and in all places to labor. . . . It has been said that a judge should not be a partizan in so far as the performance of judicial duties. I cannot accede to the proposition that it is the duty of a judge to so far forget his citizenship, and all the grand interests and duties which cluster around and adorn the relation of the citizen to the nation as to cease to feel an interest in the issues which involve the vital interests of the entire nation. . . .

But upon the judicial bench, within the *penetralia* of justice, all the exterior relations of life should be forgotten, and like the goddess whom he represents the judge should be blind to friend or foe. The sword of the law should divide unswervingly, the right from the wrong, and be wielded by an unshrinking hand.[67]

These attitudes may seem like the political posture every candidate assumes before his public, but Tourgée was sincere. He genuinely believed in the "faithful administration of the law," in the "solemn duty" every judge was "called upon to perform";[68] and in actual practice he was, unlike so many other Republican judges, neither corrupt nor venal. This was the opinion of his political opponents during his lifetime, and it is also the judgment of contemporary lawyers and historians of North Carolina. In 1944 William A. Devin summed up Tourgée's role as a judge: "With his background and temperament, with ideas in many respects foreign to those of the better element of the state, strange to say, Tourgée made an able and capable judge. He was not always dignified, but his work as a judge of law in the courts over which he presided stands out conspicuously in the judicial annals of that period. Those who intensely disliked him and all that he represented conceded his legal ability and judicial rectitude. Criticism of him has failed to suggest immorality or peculation. His private character was not attacked."[69]

In February, 1878, Tourgée published two legal volumes—*The Code of Civil Procedure of North Carolina with Notes and Decisions* and *A Digest of Cited Cases in the North Carolina*

Reports. The object of *The Code of Civil Procedure* was "to enable the professional reader more easily, quickly and certainly to ascertain what is the law in regard to practice in Civil Action Special Pleadings."[70] Both books were written for North Carolina lawyers, many of whom praised Tourgée highly for his achievement. John M. McCorkle wrote Tourgée that all of his friends found the volumes extremely useful and that *A Digest of Cited Cases* was "a work original in its conception, and I will add that in my opinion the most useful work I ever saw; you placed the Bar of North Carolina under obligations greater to you than to all others combined."[71] In recent times, a well-known judge in North Carolina has observed that "these volumes of laws, annotations and digests entailed an enormous amount of work, and they stand as a monument to [Tourgée's] tireless energy as well as to his legal ability."[72]

When Tourgée left North Carolina in 1879, he received praise from prominent Southern lawyers who had practiced in his courtroom. Some considered him "one of the ablest and fairest judges," whose arguments in court disclosed "thorough preparation and research into the Law."[73] Other men of the law—all Southerners and all opposed to him politically—praised his ability and impartiality.[74] Perhaps the clearest and most representative statement of all the personal letters sent to him at this time was written by Judge Manning: "I practised before you while you were on the bench as Judge of the District for six years. I found you always well informed, attentive, patient, and impartial. You dispatched the public business with ease and to the entire satisfaction of all the people of this Court. In fact although differing from you in politics myself, I could but admire your ability and the rapidity with which you made yourself acquainted with North Carolina decisions."[75]

IV *Outspoken Partisan*

While he was a judge, Tourgée continued to attack in newspaper articles and speeches all forms of Southern pride. From 1868 to 1870 he wrote political essays signed "Wenckar," a variation of his mother's maiden name Winegar; in these essays he denounced the Negro's inferior social status in the South and the intolerable activities of the Ku Klux Klan. In the summer of 1871, he contributed articles to the *New Berne Republican-Courier,* articles which were written by one of "God's Anynted

Phue" [God's Anointed Few], a Ku Kluxer. In these Tourgée was satirically attacking white supremacy and the caste distinctions that, as he repeatedly claimed, Southerners believed in. These examples of Southern "egotism" were later incorporated in his fiction—particularly in such novels as *A Royal Gentleman* (1874) and *John Eax* (1882).

Tourgée also aroused the enmity of Southern whites by partisan speeches delivered primarily to Negroes and concerned with such subjects as "Emancipation—considered as an historical event" or the "Next Crusade," the promising future of the Negro once he was granted equal opportunities.[76] He showed little discretion in his addresses, for he seemed to have been so intent upon making a dramatic impression on his audience that often he resorted to denigrations of local Southern heroes, denigrations which he later regretted. In North Carolina Tourgée was slightly more prudent than elsewhere; at least in his newspaper articles he concealed his denunciations of Southern leaders by using various pseudonyms, and in his public speeches he refrained from attributing crimes to individual Southern whites.

But whenever addressing people of the North, as he often did, he was completely outspoken. In the 1872 presidential campaign he delivered in Rochester, New York, a speech against Horace Greeley. In reference to past affairs in North Carolina, he charged that Zebulon Vance, while governor of the state in 1862, was "a conscript-hunter, arrested women and little children, and kept them confined in pens, had their thumbs mashed under fences. . . ." Vance denounced the charges in a letter to the New York *Tribune*, August 27, 1872. Tourgée, in a letter (undated, but probably written late in 1872), said that "no one was fool enough to misunderstand me as saying that Vance went out with gun and dogs himself to hunt conscripts . . . his subordinates did." Tourgée could have attacked no man more endeared to North Carolinians than Vance—the ex-governor was perhaps the most respected single man in North Carolina during Reconstruction. When Vance returned to power in 1877, Tourgée realized that his political ambitions were "dead."

Because of his ceaseless preference for the Negro and condemnation of the South *in toto*, Tourgée was continually threatened by the Ku Klux Klan. Attempts were made to take his life, and by 1870 the Klan was constantly following him. His experiences with the Ku Klux Klan led to an exposé of the organization, and the terror that the Ku Kluxers spread throughout the South was incorporated in his most memorable novel, *A Fool's Errand*. The exposé, called *The Invisible Empire*, was published as a factual record of Ku Klux Klan activities; it elucidated the terrifying incidents in *A Fool's Errand* in the same way that Harriet Beecher Stowe's *A Key to Uncle Tom's Cabin* commented upon the episodes in her novel.[77] It must be borne in mind, however, that Tourgée's account of the Ku Klux Klan is highly theatrical and biased. The members of the Loyal League presented in *A Fool's Errand* are all noble and upright, but the Ku Klux Klan and their friends are wicked and debased. Yet, as Stanley Horn has indicated, the League members were as guilty of bitterness as the Ku Kluxers.[78]

To the people of North Carolina, Tourgée's name became synonymous with carpetbagger, with fanatic, with Radical Republican. As C. Alphonso Smith has noted, "he was always an alien, an unwelcome intrusion, a resented imposition, a frog in your chamber, a fly in your ointment, a mote in your eye, a triumph to your enemy, an apology to your friends, the one thing not needful, the hail in harvest, the ounce of sour in a pound of sweet."[79] Smith tells of the frightened feeling and the intense antipathy that young boys like William Sydney Porter (later famous as O. Henry), growing up in Greensboro, felt for the Judge. His "residence was to the boys of the town a sort of demon's haunt. We never heard of it without shuddering," writes one man, while another remembers that "there was one house, standing far back from the street, its yard thickly shaded by elms and oaks, which to one was a place of mystery, for here lived that one-eyed scoundrel, that old carpetbagger, Judge Tourgée, the Republican boss of the State, who had sought, so we are told, to introduce social equality among negroes and whites; who had wrecked the good name and the financial integrity of our fair state by his unexampled extravagance when he was in control of the State Legislature, and who had brought about almost a reign of terror so that he was considered by all good people to be a veritable monster."[80]

With each succeeding year, Tourgée's enemies opposed him more and more. In 1873, they unsuccessfully attempted his impeachment as a judge on the grounds that he had said he wanted to expose all past Klan members and particularly desired to give Orange County "hell." On February 19, 1873, he resigned as a member of the board of trustees of the University of North Carolina because the newspapers had denounced his appointment so fiercely that he realized he might endanger the reputation of the institution. By 1874 he must have understood that his attempt to rise in North Carolina politics was futile, for in the campaign of that year, "certain of defeat," he withdrew his candidacy as judge. In addition, he lost the much-desired nomination in the fifth district for Congress.[81]

As the possibilities of an active political life in North Carolina became less real, he turned increasingly to writing. In addition to the political articles signed "Wenckar" and those addressed to "God's Anynted Phue" in 1871 and 1872, Tourgée began to write during these years a novel entitled "My Horses." The manuscript remains only in outline form, with other literary relics of this period: "the concluding chapters of a novel whose events took place in Scotland, a story of 'adventure and love'; fragmentary remains of a very long poem, dealing with cruelty to the negro; and several speeches delivered on various memorial days in the South."[82]

The largest and most impressive single work Tourgée wrote while he lived in North Carolina was a novel called *'Toinette*. He had started the manuscript in 1868-69, and when it was published in 1874 he cautiously assumed a pseudonym, "Henry Churton," so as not to endanger himself. *'Toinette*, renamed *A Royal Gentleman* in 1881, was not particularly sympathetic toward those Southerners who were then actively threatening his life. It launched Tourgée's literary career and was one of the three achievements of his life in North Carolina which he was later to recall with pride: "I do not suppose anyone who knew me would have advised me to get an election to the Convention, to accept the Judgeship, or to write ' 'Toinette'. They are the three things on which my successes are all based."[83] Tourgée was a keen critic of his own accomplishment, for in any estimation of his total work *A Royal Gentleman* deserves extensive recognition. It set the oft-repeated pattern for his later novels; it was the first work of fiction to deal directly with the problem of Reconstruction; and its sentimental description of the conflict between the Southern aristocrat and the newly liberated Negro offers an early and clear example of Tourgée's understanding—perhaps at times his misunderstanding—of post-bellum racial relations.

CHAPTER 2

The Myth of the Southern Gentleman

IN THE PREFACE to *A Royal Gentleman* Tourgée tells us
that in the summer of 1865, before the smoke of battle had
well cleared away,

> I settled near Greensboro, N. C., in the hope that a milder cli-
> mate might aid me to prolong a life somewhat shattered by the
> shock of war. My idea of Southern living was mainly derived from
> the literature of the era before the war. It is true that service
> in the army had somewhat modified it, but in the main I venture
> to say that it was a fair reflex of the idea and sentiment of the
> South; the contrast between these pre-notions and what I saw of
> the life around me, and the fresh relics of the life which had
> just passed away, impressed me keenly, and soon became of
> engrossing interest.[1]

Tourgée's claim that he traveled to the South for the purpose
of health has foundation in fact, for "his spinal wound," suffered
during the war, "the general hardship in the army, together with
a weakness of the lungs . . . had all combined to make him
anything but robust at this time."[2] But, as we have seen, Tourgée
was extremely active during this period of his life; and as soon as
he had established himself in Greensboro, he not only set up a
nursery business but became involved himself in activities which
would have exhausted a man far more healthy than he. At this
point it is worth emphasizing the partial truth—or rather the
conscious distortion—of Tourgée's statement, for throughout his
fiction and his commentaries on that fiction he omits those
aspects of his life in the South which were personally motivated;
he tends to idealize himself, to describe himself as a man who
acted on selfless intentions alone. Tourgée's journey to the South,
quite naturally, was as economically and professionally motivated
as it was physically necessary.

I *The Unconscious Influences of Slavery*

Attempting to present only a "picture of facts" in *A Royal Gentleman*, Tourgée carefully selects his characters so that they will best illuminate the whole Southern condition before and after the Civil War. These characters are meant to represent various types of the slave, the freed Negro, the slaveholder (or "royal gentleman"), and the poor-white. Figures so chosen naturally give a calculated effect to the book, but Tourgée intends to modify the dominant theme of the antislavery fiction of his time—the white man's cruelty to the Negro—and to emphasize instead Southern aristocracy, the rigid pride of caste; in so doing he feels it necessary to contrast the major types living in the South, to define the Southern condition. In later novels the question of accurate recall will be of importance—we will be concerned with what Tourgée actually remembered of the South and what he shaped to fit his own thesis. At the time he wrote *A Royal Gentleman,* however, he was deeply involved in the politics of Reconstruction and knew personally the different characters of whom he wrote.[3]

Tourgée's chief concern then is with the Southern pride of caste and tradition, deeply embedded attitudes which particularly annoyed him and other Northerners. John Trowbridge, for example, had found himself nonplussed when he faced William Gilmore Simms in 1866, and Simms asserted: "Charleston, sir, . . . was the finest city in the world; not a large city, but the finest. South Carolina, sir, was the flower of modern civilization. Our people were the most hospitable, the most accomplished, having the highest degree of culture and the highest sense of honor, of any people, I will not say of America, sir, but of any country on the globe. And they are so still, even in their temporary desolation."[4]

Tourgée, unlike Trowbridge, was not able to smile at such egotism. He maintained that this conception of Southern "civilization" and its people was largely responsible for the perpetuation of prewar attitudes of white supremacy in the post-bellum period; and his own depiction of the "royal gentleman" becomes an accounting to himself and others of the persistence of the antebellum beliefs in Negro inferiority. "The story is the delineation of a romantic sentiment," he states in the preface to *A Royal Gentleman,* "having its roots in slavery, but its flower and fruitage in freedom, and concerns itself with Slavery only in order to mark the growth of character under its influences, and show the natural and necessary sequence by which later developments arose. It carefully traces only those unconscious influences which shape and mold mental and moral qualities, and through which Slavery still lives and dominates."[5]

Other Northern writers—particularly those who were not politicians or writers for politically oriented newspapers—were not so antagonistic as Tourgée. While John W. De Forest accused the cavalier caste of "pugnacity" in *A Union Officer in the Reconstruction* and while Constance Fenimore Woolson described some of the excesses of Southern chivalry in her letters to Paul Hamilton Hayne, both authors were able to find at least partial justification for the pride of the gentry. De Forest claimed that the Southern gentleman had "begun to lose the power of thinking justly and brightly on any subject" because "slavery was established as an axiom of southern ethics and political science"; but he realized that "the chivalrous Southron" had been "too positively and authoritatively a political power to get fair treatment in literature. People have not described him; they have felt driven to declaim him; they have not preached for him or preached against him. Northern pens have not done justice to his virtues nor southern pens to his vices."[6]

Miss Woolson, far more sympathetic to the South than either De Forest or Tourgée, complained to Paul Hamilton Hayne of Southern self-esteem—"there is a height, and depth, to your pride, which actually goes beyond the comprehension of a plain Yankee like myself."[7] But in her fiction—particularly in "Rodman the Keeper," "Old Gardiston," and "King David"—she expressed an admiration for the past splendor of Southern life, as represented by the Southern gentleman; and she sympathized especially with the "plantation life, [with] the bewildering numbness of that civilization after the full import of the change was realized."[8]

Tourgée, unlike other Northern writers, had little sympathy for the Southern gentleman, and though, as Edmund Wilson has recently noted, Tourgée wants to make the point that "the Negro slaves were not treated so badly by their masters as the anti-slavery Northerners like to think . . . the ban on black blood made normal relations impossible."[9] In *A Royal Gentleman* his conception of the Southern aristocrat is Geoffrey Hunter, the son of a well-to-do lawyer in North Carolina. Hunter has all the attributes of the "royal gentleman": he is generous to his slaves and well respected by them; he is handsome, courageous, modest. In the general attitude he has adopted toward life, he has decided to be "a man, not a beast; a philosopher, not a fool"; and accordingly, he seeks "only cultivated and refining pleasures, not bestial ones."[10]

Hunter, in his ante-bellum role as the Southern gentleman, can afford to treat his slaves with extreme generosity; when the story begins, in 1858, he feels secure and content in his position as landowner. His father has given him a plantation and, at Hunter's request, the mulatto girl 'Toinette. 'Toinette is particularly desirable to Hunter, for in ante-bellum times the mulatto enjoyed higher prestige than did the pure-bred Negro. 'Toinette herself is so fair-skinned that she hardly appears to be Negro.[11]

Hunter, a young, carefree, slothful man in his early twenties, is prepared to continue in the cavalier tradition of his family. With an attractive future before him, he promises his father that he will never sell 'Toinette; to himself, he vows that he will free her when his father dies. To prepare her for her freedom, he offers the girl an elaborate education—a favor rarely granted slaves—and discovers that her intellectual capacity is extraordinary. For in addition to having a brilliant mind, her appetite for knowledge is voracious and her admiration for her mentor boundless: "Whatever precept or example [he] offered her, she seized with an amazing avidity."[12]

Tourgée pictures 'Toinette as a tender animal who "devours" the lessons of her master, who emulates him completely, who permits him to manipulate her—in a benevolent and instructive way, of course. At this point the Negro heroine is certainly far from equal to her white master, but Tourgée's implication is that her rapid progress will lead to a state of equality. His purpose in showing 'Toinette's mental ability to grasp all that her master had learned is clear: she, as a representative slave, has the capacity for intellectual progress. Her exceptional advancement dramatizes Tourgée's belief that education ought to be offered every Negro.

But though Hunter clothes and educates her as a father or husband might, he is still 'Toinette's owner and so makes her his mistress, initiating a relationship which was common among many plantation owners and Negro girls.[13] While living in the pre-Civil War South, Hunter and 'Toinette maintain a liaison which is unquestioned and tacitly accepted by everyone; and in a short time 'Toinette gives birth to a son. As Tourgée makes clear, the relationship depends on the fact that Hunter's kindness is altogether voluntary, that at a moment of the slightest irritation he can sell or demean her; he can, if he wishes, treat her as the merest chattel.

The belief in slavery that Hunter has never overtly expressed suddenly becomes very real once the war begins. He does not intellectualize the need to defend his homeland or the institution of slavery—he is simply fighting for a way of life, a way of being. Hunter, like his fellow Confederates, can hardly consider the conflict as serious: it will, of course, be won by them, and its duration will be short and bloodless. "The enemy was a myth and a jest," he thinks, "the war a pleasant picnic, and the 'Godspeed' they were receiving only an antetype of the 'welcome home,' the soldiers might expect before the autumn came and the crops were garnered."[14]

Leaving 'Toinette with their child, in whom he has taken no interest, he goes away believing that his society and his attitude toward that society will remain unchanged. But when we next see him he not only has been blinded in battle but lies close to death in a Northern hospital. 'Toinette, now a freed woman in Ohio, has further educated herself in anticipation of her lover's return. With indefatigable persistence she has sought him among the wounded; finally she and Hunter meet each other at Hunter's bedside. And now, in the most effective passages of the novel, Tourgée is able to record the effects of the Civil War on a man who had once been a non-belligerent Southerner but who cannot accept the equality of his former mistress.

Throughout Hunter's illness 'Toinette has been a tireless nurse. She has gained the affection of the other injured men, all of whom are unaware that she is a colored woman. Hunter himself scarcely recognizes the voice of his former mistress; but, when a friend describes her, praising her flawless beauty and charm, he boasts that she was once his slave. When others refuse to believe that this apparently white girl who has been serving them is actually colored, Hunter, still regarding 'Toinette as his slave, places a wager with them. He humiliates her, pretending that no war has ever been fought.

He would not cover her hypocrisy and shame. She deserved all he could make her feel for trying to pass for a white woman and a lady.

This rushed through his brain in an instant, and then, with a voice hoarse with excitement, he cried out, imperiously: "I say, you girl, Toinette! Toinette!"

Five years were brushed away in a second. Their months of toil and study were in vain. The knowledge and accomplishments for which she had striven were blotted out. The snug little home in the free North was forgotten. The love of that brave boy was obliterated. The free, white, intelligent, interesting, beautiful Mrs. Hunter was lost for the moment. In her stead was the poor, abject, timid, pretty 'nigger gal.' The old life o'erwhelmed and possessed her, like the evil spirits which entered into Magdalen. She was instantly the slave Toinette, and heard the master's voice —Marse Geoffrey's, the voice she loved—calling her in tones of angry passion. All other thought had slipped away. The world was void, except those two ideas: Marse Geoffrey; Toinette. The owner calls; the slave must answer. She saw nothing, knew nothing, heard nothing but this. The hospital, the rows of white cots, the anxious faces all staring at her, all, all, were gone. She was a chattel at Lovett Lodge again, and Marse Geoffrey in the library was calling her angrily. She started like a guilty loiterer, and answered instantly, with the inimitable and indescribable intonation of the slave:

"Sir?"

That was all she said. It was enough. It revealed all. The brand showed. The one drop of base admixture has overtopped all else, and marred the fairest hopes.

"Sir?"[15]

Hunter wins his bet, of course; but in the process he loses his pride, his caste, his status as the "royal gentleman"; he loses, in the eyes of his peers, his manhood, for he has denied his very role as the Southern aristocrat—he has taken a woman and inhumanly belittled her. Geoffrey Hunter has never had the experience of losing contests in life, and now the equal status as a human being that his former slave enjoys proves too much for him to accept.

Although obviously meant to make the reader weep, this scene has a convincing quality; it has the verisimilitude that one finds in *Miss Ravenel's Conversion From Secession to Loyalty*, when Lily Ravenel discovers that her husband, ostensibly a moral

gentleman, has actually been Janus-faced throughout a good part
of their married life. In *A Royal Gentleman* too, although the
author is more obviously writing to a thesis, a man has become
less than a human being, a man has been unable to face the one
real challenge lying outside his circumscribed life. Geoffrey
Hunter is unable to accept the social and sexual equality of
his former mulatto mistress.

Both characters are responding to their past, to their heritage.
Tourgée, by contrasting the stern command and abject answer
of his two leading figures, illustrates "those unconscious influences which shape and mold mental and moral qualities,
and through which Slavery still lives and dominates."[16] The
scene thus becomes the clearest dramatization of Tourgée's major
argument, an argument which was reiterated by him in innumerable letters and speeches during the writing of *A Royal
Gentleman* and throughout his later life. "Whatever exists by
law may be remedied by law," he maintained when trying to
explain to a friend the reasons for unfair practices against the
Negro during the post-bellum period; "but that which exists
in defiance of law rests upon a public sentiment which no
law can control."[17]

This confrontation between Hunter and 'Toinette has dramatic
truth; but it is only a moment in a rather long novel—and
Tourgée is incapable of sustaining the tension he has created.
Possessing the ability to highlight an individual scene so vividly
that it remains in the memory after the plot itself has faded,
Tourgée has little sense of continuous action. He must immediately examine his scene, interpret it, explore all of its mean-
ings, and leave nothing to our imagination; whatever emotional
truth we experience in reading such a scene is lost in Tourgée's
own verbose comments on it. As he realized, there are "splendid
things" in the book, "but there is a dead earnestness through it
all which [makes] it fall flat."[18]

In *A Royal Gentleman* we have a typical illustration of
Tourgée's inability to sustain the dramatic moment. 'Toinette
remains with Hunter despite his unforgivable treatment of her;
and, when President Lincoln appears among the wounded, she
begs him to send Hunter to a great surgeon in Washington.
Lincoln naturally agrees, and Tourgée seizes the opportunity to
write a lengthy eulogy entitled "The Poor White President,"

which, in terms of the novel's purpose, is completely inappropriate.[19]

Finally, Hunter, with his vision restored, attempts to revive what he believes was a healthy relationship with 'Toinette; he regrets that he has been so cruel to his faithful mistress and searches for her. Finding her with their son at his old plantation in North Carolina, he proposes a resumption of their antebellum life; but 'Toinette refuses: "I demand nothing from others, but I must, I will, respect myself." And his reply is the only one he is capable of making: "You presume on my love—you think me so enamoured that I will degrade myself and disgrace my family openly to obtain you. You are mistaken."[20] The incompatible forces of the newly freed, the newly educated Negro and the defeated Southern landowner are rendered in clear terms; Hunter still loves 'Toinette and regrets that she is intractable in her newly won enlightenment, but he is forced to leave her. She has become a figure in a world he does not want to understand, a menace to the sanctity of a tradition he refuses to see undermined.

Tourgée had particular difficulty in creating the final scene of his novel, for he was compelled to have his lovers part. As one critic observes, "the war destroyed the legal barriers to a union between 'Toinette and Geoffrey, but influences which Tourgée describes in his preface as 'unconscious' proved to be stronger than law."[21] That he was aware of the problem confronting him is clear from some of his introductory remarks:

> The relations between a subject and dominant race are always fruitful of romance. Inequality of rank (which may be said to culminate in the relation of master and slave) is the burden of nearly all romantic fiction. In our Southern States, since the legal status of the two races has become identical it is a task of extreme delicacy to trace the line of previous habit and note its continued strength. What the observer may clearly recognize it may be difficult to convey to the reader's mind, because the life of the present is engrafted on the root of the past—because Yesterday binds with fetters of brass Today.[22]

In a sentimental novel like *A Royal Gentleman,* one might expect the novelist to bring his lovers together to enjoy their future lives as husband and wife. But Tourgée is acutely conscious of the social and sexual relationship he is describing; Hunter was able to grant 'Toinette all the rights of a wife as long as she remained his concubine, but his sense of tradition forbade his marrying her.

In *A Royal Gentleman* the problems of Reconstruction are not explored; the attitudes of the Southern white and the Negro are examined, and Tourgée implies that these are the attitudes, "the unconscious influences," which will cause Reconstruction politicians so much difficulty. Later novels were to offer a detailed picture and interpretation of the dilemmas of Reconstruction. It is worth observing, however, that of the fiction dealing with Reconstruction *A Royal Gentleman* is one of the first works primarily concerned with a miscegenous relationship.[23] Southern authors employed the subject frequently, but none of them honestly considered the domestic problems arising from interbreeding; they were so committed to the standard conception of the "gentleman" that any elaborate examination of sexual relations with Negroes—a notoriously common occurrence in ante-bellum times—would obviously destroy their stereotyped portrait of Southern gentry. Moreover, these authors of sentimental fiction idealized the love relationship between Southern men and women to so great a degree that even Tourgée avoided emphasizing the obvious marital difficulties among whites which had been caused by the men's sexual relations with Negro slaves. Tourgée went one step further; he described his mulatto as chaste before she lived with her master and faithful to him when she became his mistress.

The Southern press censured him for characterizing the mulatto falsely, claiming that "it is very evident that the Real Purpose of Tourgée was to POPULARIZE INTERMARRIAGE BETWEEN THE RACES IN NORTH CAROLINA," by idealizing the mulatto.[24] But surely Tourgée's purpose was quite the opposite. He was strongly opposed to sexual relations between Negro and white; at the state convention in 1875 he was to introduce an amendment "making sexual intercourse between the races a misdemeanor."[25] He objected violently to cohabitation of the races because he realized that it would result in the continued suppression of the Negro. Aware that interbreeding existed in the ante-bellum South, he depicts the condition in his first novel, but miscegenation is used only so that Tourgée can indicate its unfortunate consequences. In describing the intellectual potentialities of the Negro woman and the degree to which she is capable of progressing, Tourgée is insisting that 'Toinette's mental achievements lend her a dignity and social independence that Hunter refuses to recognize.

A Royal Gentleman is Tourgée's only novel dealing with miscegenation; it is his only novel in which a Negro girl and her lover are faced with the problem of caring for their offspring. Regretfully Geoffrey Hunter leaves his child with 'Toinette at the end of the book and attempts to revive his ante-bellum life elsewhere in the South. Before the war he had intended eventually to set 'Toinette free, although of course he never wished to marry her; and now that she is politically free he still refuses to marry her, for his white friends remember their relationship and he himself will not accept her as his equal. This persistence of prewar attitudes in the post-bellum period, Tourgée maintains, is the most obvious example of "those unconscious influences which shape and mold mental and moral qualities, and through which Slavery *still lives and dominates*."[26] 'Toinette is "too proud to accept an inferior status" and "she leaves for the North again. There is no happy ending possible."[27]

II *The Poor White*

While the Negro-slaveholder confrontation is of primary importance in Tourgée's first book, the interplay of other relationships contributes to its ultimate meaning. By using—or rather misusing—an extended flashback, Tourgée attempts to acquaint the reader with the heritage of 'Toinette; he attempts to dramatize the fact that the attitude which Hunter has had toward his former mistress was a "romantic sentiment having its roots in slavery."[28] And it is through this flashback that he introduces the third character we must consider—the "poor white," Betty Certain.

The poor white, in contrast to the Negro and the slaveholder, was a figure whom post-bellum authors of the South did not care to describe. Most Southern authors after the Civil War were war-widows and daughters of poverty-stricken families of position whose reasons for writing were to earn money and to defend the ante-bellum South. Unlike these sentimental novelists, "the Northerner wrote of the trash, the freedman and those 'rascally planters,'"[29] and it was he who used clinical eyes on the South.

De Forest placed the poor white, or the "low down people" as they were called in Greenville, North Carolina, at the lowest level of society. The subtitles in his best article on the poor white, "The Low-Down People," are indicative of his general opinion: Morality, Drunkenness, Idleness, Beggary, Vagrancy, Social Degradation, Pugnacity, Ferocity, History of the Family, and Future Possibilities. Only in regard to excessive drunkenness was the poor white found innocent, and De Forest was forced to conclude: "It did not seem . . . that there was much vitality in the creature. I cheerfully leave him to the operation of the great law of natural selection."[30] Constance Fenimore Woolson shared De Forest's opinion; she could hardly tolerate the poor whites, describing them as men with "long clay-colored faces, lank yellow hair and half-open mouths," men who suffered from "ignorance and dense self-conceit."[31]

Tourgée took a totally different view; he believed that the poor white "during the next half century" would become to the fiction of the United States "what the Highlander is to Scottish literature—the only 'interesting' character in it,"[32] and his treatment of Betty Certain and other poor whites is entirely sympathetic.

But Betty Certain, far from being the only interesting figure in *A Royal Gentleman*, is the one character who least commands our attention; her actual function is to contrast the Negro as slave and as freedman, and in the role of reporter she does succeed. Recalling the relationship between master and slave in a convincing and objective way, she serves as an important commentator on the relationship between 'Toinette and Hunter. Coming to Geoffrey Hunter's home to care for 'Toinette, who has been injured by a ghost-like figure hovering about the house, she wins Hunter's friendship and recounts her past to him. She tells him that 'Toinette's mother, a quadroon called Belle, had the same relationship to her master, Arthur Lovett, as 'Toinette has with Hunter. Lovett was truly in love with his colored mistress and wished to free her from slavery; but, because of the condemnation of his community, he was forced to cease his relationship with her. Unable to free Belle and marry her in the ante-bellum South, Lovett planned on wedding poor-white Betty Certain, a woman whom he did not love but who had always been loyal to him; with Betty Certain he felt that he could at least have a marriage of affection, one based on "mutual respect."³³ The evening before Lovett's wedding, Belle, having misunderstood his relationship with Betty Certain, killed him. In the present action, Belle, in disguise, assails her daughter 'Toinette (who is also a slave to a benevolent master), fearing that she has become involved in the same inextricable relationship with Geoffrey Hunter. Failing to kill 'Toinette, she, in a state of hysteria, attacks her former lover's fiancée Betty Certain; but, when Betty overpowers her and expatiates on Lovett's difficult circumstances, Belle realizes how much she has misjudged Lovett and in remorse commits suicide.

Betty Certain thus introduces the past into the present context of the novel. 'Toinette differs from her mother not only because she is a finer, nobler human being but also because the freedom that the Civil War has afforded Negroes has granted her the opportunity to realize her potentialities. No such promise of a new life has been granted Betty Certain: she represents that Southern poor white who suffered "the scorn or indifference of the planters [and] the ridicule and scoffing of the slaves."³⁴ She has fortunately been left money by her fiancé Arthur Lovett and so is able to provide financially for herself and 'Toinette; but she nevertheless remains as much outside the social framework of the post-Civil War South as she had been in the days of slavery. Tourgée—like Thomas Nelson Page, Joel Chandler Harris, and particularly George Washington Cable (in *Bonaventure*)—sympathizes with the poor white and in *A Royal Gentleman* paints her as a pathetic regional type; but, unlike the Southern novelists, he describes her as a "living indictment, economic and moral, of the planter class."³⁵

The strength of *A Royal Gentleman* lies in Tourgée's ability to depict the attitudes and values of the slaves, the slaveholder, and the poor white. Though 'Toinette and Betty Certain were able to achieve a degree of independence, Tourgée knew too well that as long as bitter enmity was permitted to exist between slave and master, as long as Geoffrey Hunter did not accept the fact that he was morally wrong, no real solution had been effected. The most difficult problem was understanding the royal gentleman's mind; entrance into that foreign labyrinth was the first step toward an easing of racial tension. In *A Fool's Errand*, his finest achievement and his most popular work, Tourgée will come to grips with precisely that problem; the Northerner faces the South and attempts to offer it the Radical

Republican answer to post-Civil War difficulties, an answer which includes national education for all illiterates of the South. *A Royal Gentleman* presented the evolution of the problem but attempted no solution; it showed, in rather sentimental terms, the great advancement that the Negro was capable of making when offered an education. But it did not suggest what kind of education would be most satisfactory. In *A Fool's Errand*, Tourgée begins to consider his educational program; he resumes the story of Reconstruction and relates the hostility, the irreconcilability, of sectional differences that he had witnessed in Greensboro, North Carolina; and he tries to show that education is the only answer for real progress in the South. But before he was able to write his most important book, Tourgée had to finish living his foolish errand—he had to witness the demise of Radical Republicanism in the South.

CHAPTER 3

A New Career

TOURGÉE had not yet renounced all hope of advancing his political career in North Carolina. *A Royal Gentleman* failed financially, as a letter from his publishers on July 1, 1875, indicates: "only 2331 copies had been sold . . . and the loss on the edition had been about $1100."[1] Tourgée did not write another novel until 1877, when he began *Figs and Thistles* and *A Fool's Errand*; in the interim he concluded his "foolish errand" by plunging himself into local politics with as much vigor as before.

I *The Failure of Radical Republicanism*

In 1875 Tourgée was still popular enough to be elected a delegate to the second Constitutional Convention at Raleigh; and at that convention he once again played an active role. He himself was concerned with the same issues he had advocated at the convention in 1868: the equal education of Negroes and whites in separated schools; the repudiation of the state debt; the penal code; and the insistence that cohabitation of the races be outlawed.[2] But he was less successful at the 1875 convention; for, dominated by Democrats, it marked the end of Radical Reconstruction in North Carolina. Only one of the amendments which he proposed was passed, one dealing with the penal code.[3] In regard to the debt, every proposition concerning it was rejected or stifled in committee. He also failed in enacting as strong a legislation forbidding cohabitation of the races as he would have liked, for his desire to make sexual intercourse between Negroes and whites a misdemeanor was finally rejected.[4]

In many of the debates Tourgée suffered even greater defeat. On one occasion, a resolution of the judicial department had been offered to reduce the number of Supreme Court judges from five to three. The Republicans chose to regard it as an attack upon the Supreme Court; but, upon the final passage of the resolution, nineteen of them voted for it.[5]

> In the debate, many caustic allusions to carpetbaggers were made, and Tourgée came forward in their defence. He made a very heated speech and involved himself in an argument in which he was worsted. He maintained that Columbus, the Pilgrims, and even Jesus Christ were carpetbaggers. . . . Josiah Turner replied to him very effectively. Tourgée had requested that the shades might be pulled down to shut out the sunlight. Turner during his speech proceeded to show to his own satisfaction and to the discomfort of Tourgée that his parallels were not well selected. Declaring that the convention wanted light, and asking that the shades might be raised, so that the light poured into Tourgée's face, he called attention to the characteristics of the carpetbaggers and declared Judas Iscariot the original carpet-bagger if he might be judged by his character and acts.[6]

Dr. Edward Ransom, president of the 1875 convention, made various public threats to shoot Tourgée; at one time, Ransom "was waiting in the hall to attack me on my coming out, having declared to shoot me on sight." But Tourgée borrowed a revolver from a friend, walked up to Ransom in a public place, and "remained staring fixedly at him for several moments";[7] no attempt was made to execute the threat.

Tourgée knew that he had no choice but to leave Greensboro. His wife had already given birth to a daughter, Aimée, and both for the safety of his family and himself, he was forced to leave in February, 1876. It was then that President Grant appointed him Pension Agent and his wife clerk to administer oaths at Raleigh, North Carolina.[8] In the following year Zebulon B. Vance, an old enemy, was elected the first postwar Democratic governor, and the state officials were almost all Democrat. In a letter written on April 15, 1877, Tourgée described the hostility he was encountering in Raleigh:

> The truth is, that I have suffered so much in persecution and vilification at the hands of Christian bretheren [sic] that, I became convinced that it was not good for me to go to church here. I do not mean to say anything against their religion but *mine* was not robust enough to stand such a strain. I have always managed to get along somehow—I hardly know how—during the

past 12 years, until the last few months. The political feeling has
been so bitter since the election that I have quite given over
pretending to do anything but endure what I can. . . .

It is 12 years today since I first rode through the streets
on which I now look. All of that time I have lived here, yet I
have never seen an hour when political bitterness has been so
intense and hostility to Northern men so fierce as it is today. . . .
It is all I can do to live among these people now and I cannot
leave without serious loss until times improve.[9]

But in 1878 Tourgée still had political aspirations. He felt
himself popular enough to run for Congress in the Fifth Congressional District; soon, however, he realized that all of his
hopes were "dead." After failing to be elected, he wrote to his
wife on November 9, 1878: "If my vote had been a reasonable
one, I could have obtained some appointment on the strength of
it. As it is, of course, I'm dead politically, and can have no more
place in public life until I make one which must be somewhere
else."

While living in Raleigh, Tourgée did not cease his constant
criticism of the South. In 1878 he published a series of articles
dealing with the failure of Radical Republicanism in North
Carolina. These articles, signed with the pseudonym "C," and
later published as the "C" letters, denounced many local Democrats. His private correspondence reveals the great number of
people who became incensed at Tourgée's attacks on their
personal character. One E. Buck Haywood, in a letter dated
July 13, 1878, accused Tourgée of having used language "reflect-
ing upon my honor as a gentleman," and Judge Daniel G. Fowle
attacked him personally on the streets of Raleigh for his repeated
criticisms. The pseudonym had to be discarded when people
like Fowle exposed Tourgée as the author of the "C" letters.

Yet, as is true of Tourgée's journalistic writing in general, once
the reader looks behind the malicious and really puerile vilifica-
tions of individual Southern opponents, he often finds keen
assessments of Radical Republicanism. The "C" letters contain
some of the most perceptive contemporaneous descriptions of
the Republican party in North Carolina:

> The Republican party was never indigenous to Southern soil.
> In truth, it has never become acclimated there, but has remained
> from the first an exotic. A few thousand of the white people of
> North Carolina accepted it in 1868, simply as the equivalent of

CARNEGIE LIBRARY
LIVINGSTONE COLLEGE
SALISBURY, N. C. 28144

the Unionism which has always held so dear a place in their hearts. A few hundred Adullamites accepted it as the alternative of political bankruptcy and the shibboleth of political power; and a few score of earnest natives accepted it with a clear perception of its basic principles, and a *bona fide* belief in their beneficence and righteousness. A few hundred carpet-baggers received it as the spontaneous product of their native States, the sentiments for which they fought and bled. The African race in bulk received it as the incarnation and sheet anchor of that liberty which they just tested. This was the Republican party of North Carolina. Ignorance, poverty, and inexperience were its chief characteristics. That it was bitterly opposed and hated by the democracy, whose boast that it monopolized the wealth and intelligence of the State cannot be gainsayed [*sic*] by the most devoted radical, was, under the circumstances, the most natural thing upon earth. That their malignity should extend to the business and social relations of life, is hardly a matter of surprise. That it did much to verify the adage, "Give a dog an ill name and he will soon deserve it," cannot be questioned. That the old Unionists began to drop away from it as soon as they found that republicanism meant more than unionism was to have been expected. That the old should die, and the young should abandon a party which it required the faith and nerve of a martyr to adhere to, was a thing to have been anticipated. When its power began to wane, the Adullamites began to desert; the number of carpet-baggers became, by degrees, beautifully less; and only the few true believers, with a few more who still gambled for place and power against desperate odds, remained to man the water-logged bulk upon the leeshore, where she finally stranded and went to pieces more hopelessly than the *Metropolis* on the shore of Currituck.[10]

By 1879 Tourgée was convinced that the only way of avoiding the constant threats to the safety of his family and himself would be to return to the North. Though he knew that Northerners were losing interest in the problems of the South, he felt that the highly controversial fiction he planned to write in the immediate future would not be met there with the open hatred he had confronted in Greensboro and Raleigh, North Carolina. In an interview with the New York *Tribune*, September 3, 1879, he recounted his "fool's errand," and indicated why he had decided to return to the North:

A Northern man residing South is regarded as a liar by virtue of being a "carpet-bagger," all of whom are considered to be rascals and haters of the South. The Southern man is by habit and training intolerant. Excluded by slavery from the rest of the world, he learned to regard all who differed with him on any topic as necessarily criminal. Evidences of good will, sympathy, identity of interest, are all disregarded as soon as the outsider expresses a difference of opinion. . . .

The North at the close of the war, assumed that the South was what the North would have been under similar circumstances, and blundered into a scheme of reconstruction from which they expected the settlement of the differences between the whites and blacks, and, after that, a reconciliation and 'era of good feeling' between North and South. They did not know that the training and character of all Southerners made it impossible either that they should ever regard the negro as a political element, enemy or ally, or the North as anything but hostile forever; and I blame them for not knowing, and I blame myself for not knowing. I thought I could live South. In 1865 there was less bitterness than now. The rebel soldiers were yet alive, who respected their late foes and remembered the earlier days. But since then a new generation has grown up nurtured in hostility. . . .

Tourgée helped to engender the "hostility" of Southerners. The reason for his return to the North, which he indicated in personal letters to his wife, was that he had tried to make a political career for himself in the "poor, mismanaged South" and had failed; all of his humane attempts to improve the economic and social status of the Negro had met with an "intolerant resistance" that was rarely challenged by the national government. Now, with his political aspirations "dead" and with his practical efforts to aid the Negro thwarted beyond his control, he turned to fiction and began to argue his humanitarian position directly before a Northern audience.

II *Figs and Thistles*

Within a two months period—from October 4 to November 16, 1879—Tourgée published two of his more important novels, *Figs and Thistles* and *A Fool's Errand.* These books mark the two distinct directions Tourgée's fiction will take: that of pure sentimentality and that of vividly recalled history. When Tourgée

was not concerned with the political considerations in his Reconstruction novels, his manner became obtrusively sentimental.
This is the primary reason for the failure of *Figs and Thistles*;
in abandoning the South as a field for fiction, he also abandoned
a rich social milieu, a milieu that he thought was destined to be
"the Hesperides Garden of American Literature."[11] Like the
local colorists, he could not write convincing fiction of any area
he did not know intimately.[12]

The Northern setting of *Figs and Thistles* is not its only
difference from novels like *A Royal Gentleman* and *A Fool's
Errand*. More than any of his other works this book is closely
autobiographical, and Tourgée himself admitted that he had
"paid a debt of love to his childhood home."[13] Markham Churr,
the protagonist of the story, matures to manhood in Tourgée's
native state, Ohio; and, like Tourgée, he goes to college and
struggles to become a lawyer. He serves heroically for the
Union Cause and suffers a wound in the Battle of Bull Run
that almost paralyzes him. Recovering in his Ohio home, he
returns to the army and attains the rank of brigadier-general,
a position that commands the respect of all his former friends.
Thus we are again witnessing the rise of the American hero;
as Tourgée notes on his title page, this novel is "the story of an
earnest man." Once again we are reminded of Tourgée's allegiance to the long tradition of sentimental fiction that preceded
him; every sentimental novel of the Reconstruction period—or
perhaps of the nineteenth century—was to one degree or another
the "story of an earnest man."

But Tourgée's earnest young man is not entirely self-sufficient.
Like Colburne in De Forest's *Miss Ravenel's Conversion*, Markham Churr becomes the protégé of an older, more sophisti-
cated, and at times unscrupulous man. In his novel De Forest
draws the repellent portrait of a Virginia gentleman, who,
impressed by the college education and refinement of a young
New Englander, helps to advance him in the army. The gentleman, Colonel Carter—one of De Forest's "chivalrous Southrons"—
becomes involved in infidelity and graft; the virtuous New
Englander, as might be expected, emerges "pure." Shedding the
political protection that Carter has furnished him, he wins
the fair young lady of the novel, Lily Ravenel. The scenes in
which Carter goes to Washington in an attempt to "buy" his
generalship are of particular interest to us, for they throw light

on the conditions prevalent in the government at that time and, by extension, illuminate Tourgée's novel.

Boaz Woodley is the Colonel Carter of *Figs and Thistles*. He too is attracted by the honesty and intelligence of young Markham Churr and adopts him as his protégé. But the debt that Markham owes to Woodley is far greater than that owed by De Forest's hero to Colonel Carter. His home was bought by Woodley; his first success as a lawyer was due to Woodley's belief in his integrity; and, in the army, advancements were secured by Woodley. He "had been *his* captain, *his* major, *his* colonel, *his* general, and now was to be *his* Congressman."[14] Woodley's character resembles Colonel Carter's: they are unscrupulous, power-driven figures, representing the worst elements of American individualism. They are, in the end, megalomaniacs.

Markham has relied so greatly on Woodley's advice and he has let him manage his financial and personal life to such an extent that he not only finds his wife Lizzie drawing away from him, but also discovers that his every political movement is controlled by Woodley. Markham Churr discovers that, if he is to have any self-respect, he must begin by saving his own soul. The test of self-salvation comes at the climax of the book. Woodley has invested great sums of money in a transcontinental railway, and he urges Markham to support a bill that will help to increase the value of this investment. But Markham feels that his political support of such a bill can only prove detrimental to the stockholders. Despite the fact that his own money has been invested by Woodley in support of the road, he votes, after much soul-searching, against the bill.

Markham, torn between duty to Woodley and to his own moral standards, has come to learn that the moral commitment must supersede the personal obligation; for "as a man thinketh in his heart, so is he."[15] His honesty to self embitters Woodley, of course, but it recaptures the complete love of his wife. It, in effect, grants him manhood.

The relationship between Woodley and Churr is indeed a strong one, but the sentimental qualities Tourgée assigns his three main characters are so inordinate that this central motive, this central struggle, is all but suffused. Villainy and heroism are so grossly exaggerated that the contrasts are almost ludicrous. Markham's wife is idealized to the point of complete incredibility and becomes, as do all his heroines, Tourgée's reproduction of the invulnerable goddess; she is adroit, tender, and firm, as the occasion demands. Markham is an undeveloped individual, seeking self-identity and maturity, and his character is undoubtedly the best feature of the novel—but even he is too predictable. His honesty and purity of spirit are almost repugnant as we learn that "he could not remember one dishonorable act of his life. No falsehood had ever crossed his lips."[16] Boaz Woodley, his antithesis, is a wax image from the Museum of the Unreal, wherein lie all those other relics of the Gothic novel. He is the villain wearing the mask of virtue, a factitiously sinister creature whose concealed past proves to be his nemesis.

As we have seen, self-improvement inevitably becomes the cardinal characteristic of Tourgée's leading figures—self-improvement motivates their every action. But in the two novels dealing with the South that we will next examine—*A Fool's Errand* and *Bricks Without Straw*—Tourgée will not have to imagine the antagonistic force which these aspiring heroes will confront; he will not have to rely on his feeble ability to create story. The element of suspense, so necessary to an inferior author dependent upon action, will grow out of those characteristics of Southern civilization—particularly the pride of Southern people —that will form his opposing force. Tourgée knew—even if he wasn't able to take full advantage of—the ingredients for a certain kind of lasting literature; he knew that "the rise and fall of empires, the movements of races and peoples, the conflict of jarring civilizations, are the very things that most develop the elements of pathos and tragedy."[17] And despite the fact that these solid ingredients will be vitiated by sentimental excesses, a quality of reality still remains.

In *Figs and Thistles* Tourgée attempts to dramatize and personify states of mind and does not struggle with the political issues so essential to his best fiction. His characters stand on a bare stage, confront each other, and their words, their actions, must sustain the narrative. His men are involved in the Civil War, but in this case the particular conflict does not matter; any war could have suited the author's purpose as well. In addition, the society he creates is hardly defined. It is of the northern United States in mid-nineteenth century, but its geographic or temporal location scarcely affects the characters. Tourgée keeps his stage unpopulated, and for him this is artistically fatal. Markham Churr's fulfillment is foreseen from the moment we begin the novel; Lizzie Churr becomes the moral principle of the book, a creature irritatingly deified; and Boaz Woodley becomes Lucifer, fruitlessly endeavoring to make his past Hell into a present Heaven. As the book ends, we feel that the author's failure has resulted from a desertion of the materials he could best handle—those materials that appeared in *A Royal Gentleman* and that will strengthen *A Fool's Errand* and *Bricks Without Straw*. He is not concerned with the Negro, with the plantation owner, with the carpetbagger, or the white schoolteacher. He has lost his historical referents, and in the process the book becomes another one of those romances which recall the Civil War in the most standard and commonplace terms.

These criticisms, so characteristic of those that can be waged against most sentimental Civil War fiction—or against sentimental fiction in general—do not apply to Tourgée's most successful and popular novel, *A Fool's Errand*. In it he is responding to experiences he himself has just undergone and so he feels no need to invent a hero (for the hero is himself) or the villain (inevitably the Southern gentleman) or the setting—the setting is the Reconstruction South. *A Fool's Errand* has the same sentimental characteristics of *Figs and Thistles*, but at the center of the novel is an historical record that more than compensates for Tourgée's limitations as a novelist. That record, told in forceful language, is his lasting claim to a place in American letters; as Edmund Wilson has wisely pointed out, "A *Fool's Errand* was received as a sensation in its day and it ought to be an historical classic in ours—for, aside from its interests as one carpetbagger's narrative, it contains the actual text of many newspaper clippings, threatening letters and first hand testimony by victims of the Klan, and it was supplemented by a study called *The Invisible Empire*, which is a purely factual inquiry into the history of the organization, based on the author's court records and on the thirteen volumes of reports submitted by a Congressional Committee."[18]

CHAPTER 4

The Fool's Errand of
Albion W. Tourgée

IN *A FOOL'S ERRAND* Tourgée considers the attempt of a humanitarian to make real to himself and to his adversaries his aspirations for peace and equality among men. Whereas the carpetbagger is the villain of almost all Reconstruction literature, here he is the hero. In the fiction of Thomas Nelson Page (*Red Rock* and *The Red Riders*), Thomas Dixon (*The Leopard's Spots* and *The Clansman*), and Joel Chandler Harris (*Gabriel Tolliver*), those travelers who journeyed to the South in an attempt to effect political reconstruction are described as unscrupulous and even barbarous; they are obsessed by an inordinate desire for wealth, power, or fame. None of them is moderate in his feelings—none of them truly desires to improve the conditions of Negroes.

These emigrant Northerners are also the agents of whatever hostility exists between the Negroes and Southern whites. Thus Jonadab Leech in Page's *Red Rock*; Gilbert Hotchkiss in Harris' *Gabriel Tolliver;* and Simon Legree, Colonel Howle, and Alexander Larkin in Dixon's *The Leopard's Spots, The Clansman,* and *The Traitor* are all fanatical, self-centered men:

> You find the type everywhere [writes Harris]. It clings like a leech to the skirts of every movement. The Hotchkisses swarm wherever there is an opening for them, and they always present the same general aspect. They are as productive of isms as a fly is of maggots, and they live and die in the belief that they are promoting the progress of the world; but if their success is to be measured by their operations in the South during the reconstruction period, the world would be much better off without

them. They succeeded in dedicating millions of human beings to misery and injustice, and warped the minds of the whites to such an extent that they thought it necessary to bring about peace and good order by means of various acute forms of injustice and lawlessness.[1]

So exaggerated are these portraits of carpetbaggers that they bear little resemblance to their living models; these Republicans are as thoughtless of the real needs of the Negro as Simon Legree had been in ante-bellum times. The novels in which they appear are written primarily as answers to *Uncle Tom's Cabin.* The anecdote about Thomas Dixon's weeping when he saw a stage version of *Uncle Tom* in the mid-1880's and of his vowing to have his literary vengeance is one which is symbolically if not literally true;[2] it is a story which could be told of any Southern author of the late nineteenth century.

Tourgée, in contrast to most writers of Reconstruction literature, presents a carpetbagger who is more sinned against than sinning, who is guileless and selfless and tolerant. And when he fails because of his innocence, Southerners and Northerners alike deride him. This novel "is the narrative of one of Folly's failures," Tourgée writes in his preface. "The hero can lay no claim to greatness. A believing Noah there is in it, a well-built ark, and an indubitable flood. But the waters prevailed, and the Fool went down, and many of the family with him. The Wise Men looked on and laughed."[3]

So deeply had Tourgée responded to his Southern experiences that he was compelled to document in stark terms his indictments not only of Southern cruelty toward the Negro but also of Northern complacency, and his remorse over the failure of Reconstruction is here epitomized as it is nowhere else in his later works. The novel serves as the encyclopedia of all his most cherished ideas and ambitions. In writing the book, he was careful to point out that "the one merit the story claims is that of honest, uncompromising truthfulness of portraiture. Its pictures are from life. And even in this which he boasts as a virtue may be found, perhaps, the greatest folly committed by One of the Fools."[4]

But Tourgée's characterization of his own novel is far from accurate, for the "pictures" he chose to include in *A Fool's Errand* are carefully selected. We do not see the young carpet-

bagger who moved into North Carolina and immediately antagonized the people with his exaggeration of Southern crimes;
nor do we see the unscrupulous Tourgée who delivered speeches
denouncing national leaders such as Andrew Johnson or who
descended to journalistic slanders (in the "C" letters) of prominent Southerners like Judge Daniel G. Fowle. We see instead
a humane Northerner, who because of innocuous and selfless
attempts at improving the Negro's plight, is condemned by the
uncompromising and reactionary Southerner.

I An Independent Northerner

The title *A Fool's Errand* was chosen to set the tone of the
entire novel. Tourgée's idealistic Northerners who came to the
South with liberal ideas, reinforced by their victory in the Civil
War, were bound on "a fool's errand." They had their answers
before they left their Northern homes; and, though they expected
a reasonable amount of resistance, they had no idea of its
extent. They intended to bring the Negro religion, a better
standard of living, and, above all, education. But they suffered
from intellectual pride, as Tourgée acknowledged when he wrote
A Fool's Errand; for they ignored the valuable contribution
that the Southern whites might have made to the education of
the freedman. Consequently, the Southerners resisted these
humanitarians and thought of them as pernicious influences.
The tension and hostility that existed between Northerner and
Southerner were unrelieved, and the sufferer was the Negro. "The
North was inclined to be impatient, to insist upon an immediate
solution. The South in the face of the constant pressure and
menace of power from outside throughout the Reconstruction
period failed to admit that there was any problem except to
reassert control by the white man. Meanwhile, the Negro, 'drunk
with freedom' and the football of Reconstruction politics, was
largely unfitted for progress by the noise made over him."[5]

Yet Tourgée insisted that the Negroes learned that their
interests were antipathetic to those of the Southern whites and
that they acquired such knowledge from Northern teachers,
missionaries, and organizers of Negro churches; from traveling
politicians; and from Union soldiers.

The Northerners' mission of salvation was an unequivocal
failure, but Tourgée realized too that their folly was not entirely

ludicrous. These men were men of faith; and so, despite the futility of their attempt to reconstruct the South, they became the superior individuals of the nation. They were the imaginative men of their generation, Tourgée felt; and, as always, they were traduced by those who did not know courageous belief. "The life of the Fool proper is full of the poetry of faith," Tourgée wrote in his preface. "He may run after a will-o'-the-wisp, while the Wise deride; but to him it is a veritable star of hope. He differs from his fellow-mortals chiefly in this, that he sees or believes what they do not, and consequently undertakes what they never attempt. If he succeeds in his endeavor, the world stops laughing, and calls him a Genius; if he fails, it laughs the more, and derides his undertaking as A FOOL'S ERRAND."[6]

The fool in Tourgée's novel is Comfort Servosse, who goes to the South with his young wife and child to improve his health. A naturally volatile and ebullient man, he naïvely feels that "manufactures will spring up, immigration will pour in, and it will be just the pleasantest part of the country."[7] But his wife Metta, whose name is a half-anagram for Emma Tourgée, fears that life among the rebels will prove dangerous; and Servosse, heeding her warning, writes for advice to his former college president, the Reverend Enos Martin, a staunch abolitionist before the war. The Reverend, who is modeled on Martin B. Anderson, the president of Rochester College when Tourgée studied there, suggests that it is "only by . . . intermingling of the people of the two sections that they can ever become one, and the danger of the future be averted."[8] Metta's personal fears are unassuaged by this political generalization, but Servosse is determined and she finally acquiesces. He buys a despoiled plantation in Warrington, North Carolina, and prepares to practice law there.

But, from the moment he arrives in the South, he experiences hostility. A lawyer pleading a case—his own, as we see—Tourgée presents scene after scene as evidence of the South's hatred toward the newcomers.[9] Servosse and his wife invite to a Thanksgiving dinner six New England women who have come to North Carolina to teach Negro children and to help reduce the high rate of illiteracy. These women, as Servosse's wife writes her sister, "are employed by the Missionary Association to teach in the colored schools that have sprung up all over the South like magic, and are really 'missionaries' in the very best sense of the word. They are from six different States, and never saw each other until they met here at the school in Verdenton, and are all cultivated, refined ladies of the best class of our Northern people, who have come here simply to do good."[10] The next week Servosse dismally reads the local newspaper's vindictive commentary that he "had all those free-loving nigger missionaries of the female persuasion out at Warrington to celebrate the new Yankee holiday, which has been added to the governmental calendar since the first of Lincoln's reign, called Thanksgiving Day. The day itself is a relic of New England Puritan hypocrisy. . . . Colonel Servosse cannot expect his family to be recognized by respectable people if he chooses such associates for them."[11]

This incident, which first arouses Southern enmity because of Servosse's open sympathy for the Negro, is important in the development of Tourgée's attitude toward public education. During his fourteen-year residence in North Carolina, Tourgée was concerned with the most immediate and effective method of primary education possible; consequently, in the mid-1860's— the period which Tourgée is describing in the first section of A Fool's Errand—he strongly supported those Northern teachers who had come South to teach Negroes, feeling that these educators were sincere and dedicated. Actually they were attracted to the South for both altruistic and selfish reasons; some of these were "religious and humanitarian interest and abolitionist experience, desire for improvement of financial status, search for health, previous vocational connections, and love of adventure."[12] The intelligent Southerner—and not the outspoken racist whom Tourgée presents—objected to these Northerners, for he felt that they regarded the South as a missionary field and that they had come on "a sort of second invasion." An editorial in the American Freedman stated that "the South no longer opposes the education of the freedman. This it approves—it even attempts to provide. But it looks askance on Northern interference. Its hostility is excited not by the school-marm, but by the Yankee school-marm."[13] Southern hostility toward Northern teachers was understandable, for the Southerner felt that these teachers were supported and manipulated by Radical Republican reconstructionists like Tourgée; and, in most cases, they were.[14]

In A Fool's Errand Tourgée describes his hero as a humanitarian who is simply hospitable to these missionaries but who in no way wishes to control them. Servosse and his wife take on their religious views and begin to see their life in the South as one of dedication to a humanitarian cause: "when we knelt for our evening prayer," Servosse's wife comments, "I did thank God with all my heart that he had directed our steps hitherward, for I believe we have a blessed work to do, and that our lives here will not be in vain."[15] Soon Servosse establishes a Sabbath school for the colored people near his home, builds houses for Negroes, sells them land, and assists them in purchasing stock. He receives further condemnation and becomes an object of unmitigated hatred; in his desire to reconstruct the Negro, he incurs the wrath of white Southerners who wish to perpetuate the rigid caste system of ante-bellum times.

Unaware of the deep-seated resentment before he arrived, Servosse now has met it face to face and knows that he cannot leave until he has somehow attempted to ameliorate conditions. He senses that he is witnessing evils that stem from a fallacious belief in white supremacy, but the complex problems of Reconstruction have not become clear, and true understanding of them lies far in the future. "He had never been anything of a politician," Tourgée claims, "and had no expectation of being one";[16] yet his interest in public affairs—like that of his prototype —is insatiable, and he attends a political meeting devoted "to the general interests of the country." At this meeting he is characterized by Southerners as a man "in favor of social equality, nigger witnesses, nigger juries, and nigger voters";[17] but, in spite of his minority position, he is urged to speak, to offer his political views.

Unable to appreciate or tolerate the reasons for the white man's bitterness toward the Negro and the carpetbagger, Servosse antagonizes his Southern listeners by insisting on equal rights for all races. He advocates gradual Negro suffrage, telling the people that if they give "the elective franchise to every colored man who owns a hundred dollars' worth of real estate, and everyone who can read or write"[18] the nation will be satisfied. He soon learns, however, that not only does he have to restrain himself from expounding new ideas, but also that he cannot oppose any of the well-established traditions of the civilization surrounding him. His life is threatened by some of those who have listened to his speech, but he is warned in time by a militant Negro Jerry Hunt, familiarly called Uncle Jerry, a character based on one of the actual Negro leaders of the Union League, Wyatt Outlaw.

Despite Southern resistance to his ideas, Servosse refuses to be intimidated by the threats of Southern whites. When he inexorably condemns Southern cruelty toward the Negro and the Negro's helper, he receives letters warning him of death to others who have also tried to help the colored man. These letters, which closely parallel those received by Tourgée himself, are sent not only by hardened racists but by friendly Southerners who fear any further violence between the conflicting forces in the South. Unionists—those Southern men who sympathized with the North during the war—tell him "that he is a brave man; but no one would any more have uttered such sentiments as he puts out . . . the danger was so apparent."[19] Tourgée consistently and foolishly condemns these people, and he praises his hero's audacity and courage in stating his position so forthrightly:

> How he [Servosse] dared to stand up and maintain ideas at variance with the accepted creed of that class of men who had always formulated and controlled public opinion, they could not understand. They hated secession, always had hated it; they had voted against it in 1861; some had been outspoken against it on the stump, in the street, everywhere, and at all times: but in the main the opposition had been a silent one. The terrible suppressive power which slavery had exercised over liberty of thought and speech had grown into a habit of mind. Men who for generations had been unable to express their thoughts above a whisper, as to one of the institutions by which they were surrounded, became cautious to the verge of timidity. Many a time did our Fool listen to the approval of men who would glance cautiously around before addressing him, and then say in a low, hushed tone,——
>
> 'That is what we want. I tell you it did me good to hear you; but you must look out! You don't know these people as I do. It don't do to speak out here as you do at the North.'[20]

Servosse refuses to heed these various admonitions; he continues, in an even more aggressive manner, to champion the rights of the Negro. One of his servants informs him of the growth of the Union League and the need the members have of learned leaders. Servosse agrees to attend a meeting, one which Tourgée describes sympathetically at some length. Servosse meets some of the important leaders of the League and particularly a rabid scalawag, John Walters, who is modeled after Senator John W. Stephens, an outspoken leader of the Negroes, who was murdered by the Ku Klux Klan on May 21, 1870. Walters, as radical as Servosse himself, is intolerant of any vacillation on the part of members of the Union League. He sharply criticizes the president of the League, a figure patterned after the Provisional Governor, William W. Holden, claiming that he was untrustworthy during the war. He isn't dangerous, "but he was everything to all men during the war, and will be anything to anybody until the end of time if it will butter bread for Tommy Sanderson [Holden]."[21]

Servosse, who soon becomes known as a leader of the Union League, is responsible to a great extent for disciplining and organizing the Negroes and consequently, for curbing the power of the native Southerners. In his description of the Union League, Tourgée emphasizes only those humanitarian aspects of the organization. He refrains from illustrating its operations or Servosse's specific activities, and the final impression is of a defenseless group of people maligned and abused by white supremacists. Actually members of the League

> were pledged to uncompromising and unconditioned loyalty to the Union, to complete subordination of political views to this loyalty, and to the repudiation of any belief in states rights. . . . It [the League] was one of the first organizations to declare for negro suffrage and the disfranchisement of Confederates; it held steadily to this declaration during the four years following the war; and it continued as a sort of bureau in the radical Republican party for the purpose of controlling the negro vote in the South. Its representatives were found in the lobbies of Congress demanding extreme measures, endorsing the reconstruction policies of Congress, and condemning the course of the President [Johnson].[22]

Ironically many of the League's customs, rituals, and methods resembled those of the Ku Klux Klan. The League's password consisted of various hand motions which were accompanied by pronouncement of the "Four L's": "Liberty," "Lincoln," "Loyal," and "League."[23] "Anonymous warnings were sent to obnoxious individuals, houses were burned, and notices were posted at night in public places on the houses of persons who had incurred the hostility of the order."[24]

Later in his life, Tourgée defended the activities of the Union League, claiming that it was organized solely for the purpose of self-defense:

> It is enough to make a cast-iron dog laugh to read the tales of atrocities committed by the "Union League" as it was called. I suppose I know as much about it and its workings as any man ever did. It was the most harmless of voluntary associations. It was organized in Philadelphia early in the war and was intended simply as a means of enabling the loyal people of that section to make themselves known to our soldiers. Colored people were afterwards admitted to it for the purpose of enabling them to give notice to each of the Ku Klux raids. It tolled bells and lighted beacon fires when the ghostly horsemen appeared. I canvassed the whole State in the spring of 1868, and know I suppose, all there was to be known of such an organization. I never heard in any of its meetings anything but the mere expression of patriotic sentiment.[25]

Such innocent behavior can hardly be attributed to the members of the league. Negroes belonging to the Union League did steal and at times murder. "Stealing on the part of the Negro seemed to have been a heritage from his past life conditions. He had brought from slavery a sort of childish want of respect for property. . . . Murder also was a crime frequently committed by Negroes. The victims were often men of the white race, whom they killed to obtain money. . . . The act was perpetrated with an unusual degree of atrocity."[26] As Stanley F. Horn has noted, "'the depredation of the Loyal League encouraged the antagonistic force of the Ku Klux Klan. The sight of armed Negroes meeting in secret conclaves filled the Southerners with a shuddering fear."[27] The Ku Klux Klan, rather than the League, was the defensive organization—at least when it was first formed in North Carolina in 1868.

II *The Growth of the Ku Klux Klan*

Tourgée continues to attribute to his hero a political innocence he himself did not possess. In actuality Tourgée sought the nomination to the state convention and eagerly participated in its activities. Servosse, on the other hand, assumes a position that "no one seemed to desire," one "which promised to be onerous, without honor, and of little profit; which it was felt would cast odium upon the individual, and social and religious ostracism upon his family."[28] He proposes at the state convention six basic reforms for the solution of Reconstruction problems and thus "becomes an outlaw in the land where he hoped to have made a home, and which he desired faithfully to serve."[29] These projected reforms, identical with those suggested by Tourgée himself at the Convention in 1868, consist of

1. Equal civil and political rights to all men.
2. The abolition of property qualifications for voters, officers, and jurors.
3. Election by the people of all officers—legislative, executive, judicial—in the state, the counties, the municipalities.
4. Penal reform: the abolition of the whipping-post, the stocks, and the branding-iron; and the reduction of capital felonies from *seventeen* to one, or at most two.
5. Uniform and *ad valorem* taxation upon property, and a limitation of capitation tax to not more than three days' labor upon the public roads in each year or an equivalent thereof.
6. An effective system of public schools.[30]

Such reform measures, as Servosse soon observes, are ideal and cannot be accomplished by their mere enactment. How far they are from realization he quickly learns, for throughout the South the Ku Klux Klan has struck, attacking the colored man, repressing liberal carpetbaggers, and evincing an unwillingness to accept any post-bellum social framework that involves the abdication of the Southern "cavalier."

If Servosse has not understood the problems facing the Reconstructionists heretofore, the Ku Klux Klan and Servosse's few liberal North Carolinian friends make the pride and independence of the Southerner unforgettably patent. "We are poor now," one of his liberal friends, Nathaniel Hyman, claims. "[We] have lost everything but honor; I hope we shall not lose that."[31] The Ku Klux Klan, on the other hand, terrorizes and browbeats Negroes who seek to establish their own business or their own careers in life, and it attacks those neighbors (such as Nathaniel Hyman's son) who befriend Servosse and other carpetbaggers.

As Tourgée tells us in *The Invisible Empire*, the supplementary work to *A Fool's Errand,* the Ku Klux Klan was at first considered by Northerners to be a huge hoax that Southerners were playing on the Negroes. No one took the adolescent terrorism seriously; but, as lynching of "rising" colored men, Negro school teachers, and Radical Republicans became rife, the country knew that the Ku Klux Klan was an active manifestation of exaggerated Southern pride. And Comfort Servosse, living in a state whose early affairs in regard to the Ku Klux Klan "had followed the usual pattern of the period,"[32] experiences the machinations of the Invisible Empire from the date of its first activities in 1868.

Tourgée's description of the Ku Klux Klan is biased and not wholly accurate historically. The early Klan was largely an outgrowth of a belief on the part of Southerners that the reconstruction policies were totally intolerant and could not be suffered by them. It was encouraged to a great extent by the unscrupulous activities of the Loyal League, of which Tourgée was an important leader in 1866 and 1867, and by the advent of Radical Republicanism and Negro supremacy. "It is not surprising," writes Stanley F. Horn, "that the white people should come to feel that some sort of organization for self-protection was needed, and throughout the South there began spontaneously to spring up local defense groups, generally in the form of secret societies, designed primarily to offset the aggressiveness of the Loyal League. . . . As the Ku Klux Klan, with its awesome name, began to gain in fame, these scattered, informal loyal organizations began to see in it the possibility of a widespread secret society which could carry on this defensive work in the South in a most effective manner."[33]

Tourgée's representation of the Ku Klux Klan in *A Fool's Errand* is only partially correct, for he refuses to admit that the organization was responding to the excesses of Negroes and carpetbaggers. He fails to emphasize the importance of the Union League, and one is led to believe that the Ku Klux Klan wishes only to suppress the purely selfless motives of Radical Republicans like Servosse. Moreover, Servosse himself hardly resembles Tourgée in that he never descends to denunciations of particular Southerners; he never makes speeches which exaggerate Southern oppression of the Negro; he never writes articles nor edits newspapers which, because of their constant criticism of the Southern attitude toward the Negro, incite local citizens to take retaliatory measures. Servosse is always above the political battle in which his living model was intensely—and disastrously—embroiled; he possesses only the altruistic motives which formed a part, though admittedly a significant part, of Tourgée's attitude toward the Negro. Servosse is a passive hero, and the later Klan which Tourgée describes consists primarily of uncompromising racists. Thomas Nelson Page in *Red Rock* draws a more reliable account of the Klan's evolution, but in Page's work the Ku Kluxers are too noble and too "gentlemanly," and the Klan is viewed as only defensive. Neither Radical Republican nor Southern apologist was able to judge such a controversial phenomenon as the Ku Klux Klan realistically without compromising his own political point of view.

Servosse becomes aware of the Klan's activities when he hears the story of Bob, an imaginative Negro who has attempted to break the bonds of serfdom by opening his own blacksmith's shop. Refusing to do work for a white man who has not paid his bills, Bob is told that he is becoming independent and too "smart"; and, when he receives a threatening notice from the Ku Kluxers, his attempt at genuine independence is finally destroyed by the Invisible Empire. The last few sparks of his once bright ambition fade into nothingness as he recounts his defeat to Servosse, as he stands helplessly before the Fool: "But ef men can come to his [the Negro's] house in de middle ob de night, kill his baby an' beat an' abuse him an' his family ez much ez dey please, jes' by puttin' a little black cloth ober der faces, I may ez well give up, an' be a slave agin."[34]

The massacres committed by the Ku Klux Klan become so frequent that Servosse soon loses faith in the ineffectual government and feels that the only answer left the victims of aggression is retaliation. He tells the Negro Bob that "a man has a right to protect himself and his family; and, if our government is too blind or too weak to put down this new rebellion, there are only three courses before us—you and me, and those who stood with us: the one is to fight the devil with fire—to kill those who kill—guard the fords, and, whenever we see a man in disguise, shoot him down; another is to give up everything else for the privilege of living here; and the third is to get away."[35]

Servosse's choice is rendered inevitable by the increased violence of the Ku Klux Klan. Tourgée's description of the Klan is artistically clumsy, but because of this very clumsiness the growth and threat of the Klan are the most moving and impressive sections of the novel. The individual scenes seem at first only tenuously connected, but soon the reader discovers that the central, tough strand running through them is Tourgée's sincere and bitter hatred of the organization. The formlessness of the description parallels and faithfully mirrors the chaotic nature of Reconstruction itself.

Tourgée cites case after case as evidence of the Klan's inhumanity, tracing its rise and "triumph through blackmail, bullying, flogging, rape of women, castration of men, contemptuous violence to children, burning of Negro houses and shootings, stabbings, drownings and hangings of anybody who [offers] serious resistance."[36] Jessie Hyman, the son of Servosse's friend, is whipped by the Klan because of his sympathy for the Negro and the carpetbagger, and Servosse sends him away from the South, certain that he will not be safe among so many aroused militants who especially loathe the scalawag. His fear for Hyman is justified; in a short time two of the most horrendous murders during the Reconstruction in North Carolina are committed: that of the Unionist John Walters and the Negro leader Jerry Hunt.

Tourgée has selected these two outrages to strengthen his book as a valid contemporaneous account of Reconstruction in North Carolina. They are based on famous acts of aggression by the Ku Klux Klan—the murders of Senator John W. Stephens and Wyatt Outlaw—and no two examples Tourgée could have selected would have better proved the point that the Ku Klux Klan was totally lawless. These murders, hardly fictionalized, illustrate how forceful and persuasive a writer Tourgée can be when he stays close to recorded fact. The murder of Walters— a scandal throughout the state, which Ku Kluxers unsuccessfully try to suppress—is caused by Walters' outspoken animosity of those Southerners who attempt to deny education to the Negro: "he was very bitter in his denunciation of the slave-holding aristocracy, and would persist in declaring that they had starved the souls of the poor people, and kept them from the tree of knowledge, just to promote their own selfish aims, and enhance their own health. It's the only thing I've ever heard John Walters grow eloquent upon . . . but I've heard him sometimes on the stump when he seemed to get out of himself, and be another man, in the wild eloquence with which he urged the need of education, and deplored the manner in which he had been robbed of its privileges and advantages."[37]

Walters was loved and admired by the Negroes so that, when they hear of his death, they are "as distressed as if [they had] lost a brother."[38] They search for his body and find it in a room in the courthouse, in the same place that the body of Stephens, his prototype, was discovered: "There, pressed down into a box, with a pile of firewood heaped upon him, a stab in his throat, and a hard cord drawn taut about his neck, stark and cold, was the body of John Walters—the Radical! There was very little blood in the room, only a few drops on the floor, and *one drop on the window-sill!* The stab in his throat had cut the artery. Where was the blood? The physician who examined the body said he must have bled internally."[39]

Servosse's disaffection with those measures he had once propounded is climactically crowned by a second brutal murder, the lynching of the leader of the Negroes, Uncle Jerry, the most fearless opponent of the Ku Klux Klan.[40] Convinced that it is better to perish in resisting these truculent oppressors than to live under their domination, Jerry urges his fellow colored men to organize. But the Negro has known too much fear of his master and is not prepared to support overtly agitators like Uncle Jerry. Denouncing the Ku Klux Klan at a prayer meeting (after three Ku Kluxers, sitting at the meeting, have mocked the humble Negroes), Jerry and his community surprisingly experience no repercussions for a few days. But less than a week later the fateful visit is made: "Gathering in twos, they fell into ranks with the regularity and ease of a practiced soldiery, and, as they filed on towards Verdenton, showed a cavalcade of several hundred strong; and upon one of the foremost horses rode one with a strange figure lashed securely to him."[41]

On Sunday, the day after the lynching of Jerry, Servosse visits the town and witnesses the unforgettable sight: "Upon the limbs of a low branching oak not more than forty steps from the Temple of Justice, hung the lifeless body of old Jerry."[42] Helpless in the hands of men they cannot identify, fearful because they might be the next assailed, the Negroes cringe, lose heart, and keep silent the thought that only one bystander dares express: "It don't do fer niggers to *know too* much! Dat's what ail Uncle Jerry!"[43]

Whereas at one time Servosse imagined that opposing forces

would halt the scourge of the Ku Klux Klan, he knows now that such an attempt is futile. The militarily trained members attack only at night and are always masked. In addition, it is almost impossible to identify any one of them; for they are not, as one might think, only delinquent citizens; in some cases they are actually the most respected and cultured of Southerners.[44] Men like Servosse were to be constantly surprised at discovering that their placid local lawyer or doctor was as devoted a Ku Kluxer as the most obvious belligerent. The Fool feels himself a bewildered child, lost in a kind of frightening, surrealistic maze of Southern life; all exits seem to be only *culs de sac*.

But Tourgée, by eliminating essential information, has failed to render an "honest, uncompromising truthfulness of portraiture" and has thus created the impression that his hero is intolerably treated by the proud villains of Southern culture. The Ku Kluxers are all grotesque exaggerations, and Servosse is an unreal model of selflessness. Those Southerners who murdered John Walters and Uncle Jerry are accurately described, but Tourgée leaves the unfair impression that they represent the sentiments of most Southerners. As North Carolinian John M. McCorkle remarked soon after the book was published, Tourgée took "intense and exceptional southern types as indices of the familiar, everyday life of the South."[45]

The description of the Ku Klux Klan in the fiction of Reconstruction is a particularly good illustration of Tourgée's fundamental differences from Southern authors. In the novels of Page, Harris, and Dixon, the Klan is a defense against a "group of pot-house politicians" who "attempt to wipe out the civilization of the South."[46] In Page's *Red Rock* (1898) the hero is a Klan leader, but he does not countenance violence; he informs his Northern lover that "there are no Ku Klux here—there never were any—except for a little while . . . and there is not one in the County or in the South who would do you an injury, or with whom, if you were thrown, you would not be as safe as if you were guarded by a regiment."[47] The Southern gentleman resorts to the Ku Klux Klan only to suppress carpetbaggers and insurgent Negroes; and he objects to the later Klan, "a cowardly body of cutthroats," asserting that it is "no longer the old organization which . . . had acted for the public good, and with a high purpose."[48] Similarly, in Harris' *Gabriel Tolliver* (1902) "the Knights of the White Camellia" are organized to defy the Union League, to disturb "the meetings of Negroes";[49] in Dixon's *The Leopard's Spots* (1902), Klan members protect Southern civilization from "African barbarism"—they act only in self-defense; and the Ku Klux Klan becomes "the answer to their foes of a proud and indomitable race of men driven to the wall."[50]

Tourgée describes, in *A Fool's Errand*, a Klan comprised of frightened Southern racists who murder outspoken Negroes. As far as it goes, Tourgée's description is accurate. But Tourgée selects his facts—as do the Southern authors—to fit the point of view he is representing. The reader does not have the impression, while reading *A Fool's Errand*, that there were many Klansmen who objected to any violence. Those gentlemen admired by Tourgée are the Southerners who finally renounce the Klan and accept the equality of Negroes.

The various acts of aggression against the scalawags Jessie Hyman and John Walters and the Negroes Bob and Uncle Jerry are a dramatically impressive introduction to the climax of Tourgée's story—Servosse's personal abuse by the Ku Klux Klan. Tourgée and his family had witnessed these ravages of the Klan; and, as Edmund Wilson points out, "the story of the nightmarish movement, gradually making itself felt and closing in on the incredulous Northerners, was the one really valuable book Tourgée had it in him to write."[51]

Servosse's sympathy for these maligned people has encouraged the antipathy of native Southerners so that he is increasingly threatened by Klan members. At this point in the novel Tourgée is following closely the attempts that had been made on his own life. The Klan had considered his own removal in the early months of 1870, and "the death sentence was about to be passed when an influential leader of the Klan, coming late, appeared. As soon as he was informed of the state of affairs he interfered, and after much persuasion succeeded in having the decree reversed."[52] Letters, anonymous and undated, had also warned Tourgée: "Dear Sir, This is to inform you to hold no more Courts in Carolina you have had your day if you ever hold another or attempt it you will share the fate of Mr. W. Stevens [Senator John W. Stephens, murdered by the Ku Klux Klan on May 21, 1870] it is ordered you leave the state. . . . by order of the KKK." In a letter written on May 26, 1870, Tourgée commented on Senator Stephens' death and said, apprehensively, "I should not be at all surprised if I were the next victim."[53]

Tourgée is now reporting more than rendering in fictional terms the events that occurred to him. Directly after the murder of Uncle Jerry, Servosse writes a letter which recounts all the injustices inflicted on Negroes and Republicans in North Carolina, and he addresses it to "a Wise Man [a Northern politician] with whom he has maintained such intimacy of relation as folly may be allowed to hold with wisdom." Tourgée tells us: "This letter, for some reason or other, though it was a private one to himself, the Wise Man allowed to be published in the newspapers: so it resulted that the Fool received more than one answer thereto."[54]

The background of this letter, which played so crucial a part in Tourgée's—and therefore Servosse's—role in Reconstruction, reveals how oppressed Tourgée felt and clearly suggests how closely his own experiences match those which appear in his fiction. In the summer of 1870 Governor Holden published a personal letter of Tourgée, which had attacked the Ku Klux Klan for its outrages on the Negroes and had specified particular cases of its crimes. This letter—written to Senator Abbott, another carpetbagger and the "Wise Man" to whom Servosse writes in *A Fool's Errand*—supported Holden's claims that the state was in a condition bordering on insurrection. As published in the New York *Tribune*, the letter declared that the Ku Klux Klan had broken into four or five thousand houses, that they had burned fourteen houses in Tourgée's immediate district, and that he knew of thirteen murders in the district. This letter was used with telling effect, without comment from Tourgée; "but after the Radicals had gained the full benefit of its contents and the election was over, he blandly stated that it had been misquoted. 'I wrote four arsons instead of fourteen,' he said. 'Instead of 4,000 or 5,000 houses opened, I wrote 400 to 500. I said thirteen murders in the state, not in the district.' Incidentally, it was later found that three of the men reported murdered were still alive; and it was also stated that some of the house-burnings and other acts of violence were perpetrated by Holden's supporters to provoke resistance to the exaggerated Ku Klux menace."[55]

Tourgée was infuriated with Holden for publishing the letter. On September 5, 1870, he wrote to a friend: "Holden made a series of mostly egregious blunders, and then tried to pack it off on me by publishing my letter which had been put into his hands under a promise express of secrecy."[56] Tourgée's reference to Holden's "blunders" was accurate, for during the summer months Holden had used every possible means to suppress the Ku Klux Klan. On June 20, Holden had appointed George W. Kirk, an ex-Union soldier, to command occupation troops which had been organized to control the allegedly insurgent Klan; and on July 15, Alamance County was occupied. The state elections were to be held on August 4; and Democrats charged, with complete justification, "that Holden was using martial law to carry the August elections."[57] Holden knew that "if the intimidation tactics [of the Ku Klux Klan] were not suppressed, the Negroes could scarcely be expected to cast their ballots for [his] party."[58] Tourgée's letter was used by Holden as proof of the Klan's depredations in the state.[59] Several weeks after the election, in a letter to a committee appointed by the Guilford Bar to inquire into the "authorship of a certain letter" published under Tourgée's signature, Tourgée again denied the accuracy of the letter as printed in the *Tribune*.[60]

Tourgée and Holden shared the same political position during Reconstruction, but they differed in methods of administration. In August of 1870 Tourgée expressed dissatisfaction with Holden as governor. He had urged Holden to put detectives to work to apprehend the Ku Klux Klan in Alamance: "I am confident that with two or three of these I could easily arrange to detect and capture a crowd *en masque* in a month, whom it would be impossible to acquit by any sort of chicanery or perjury. They must however be caught in the very act with all their paraphernalia upon them in order to punish them. It is the only plan I can suggest, and I think it is the cheapest one that can be easily adopted."[61]

But Holden largely ignored Tourgée—only two detectives were employed in February, 1870 [62]—and in a letter dated August 17, 1870, Tourgée wrote to a friend, E. S. Clark, that "in my opinion he [Holden] is a first class bungler. If we had only had a man of affairs . . . at the Executive helm this Ku Klux revolution could never have taken place. . . . As a Republican, of course, I support him as far as I can. . . ." When Holden permitted Tourgée's private letter to be published in the New York *Tribune* on August 3, 1870, Tourgée lost complete faith in the governor and wrote to him, probably late in 1870,

"I repeat again, my entire confidence in your official integrity and purity of motive, except so far as your conduct may be colored by a persistent determination not to abandon an opinion or yield to conviction—which in its results may approximate very closely to injustice."[63]

In *A Fool's Errand* Tourgée does not suggest the political motives for publishing the letter nor does he suggest his—Servosse's—deep personal irritation at its appearing in a Northern journal. The letter was a turning point in Tourgée's career as a carpetbagger—it is one of the most direct causes of Servosse's confrontation with the Ku Klux Klan. As Tourgée writes:

> The Fool's neighbors having read his letter to the Wise Man, as published in the great journal in which it appeared, were greatly incensed thereat, and immediately convened a public meeting for the purpose of taking action in regard to the same. At this meeting they passed resolutions affirming the quiet, peaceful, and orderly character of the county, and denouncing in unmeasured terms all reports or rumors to a contrary purport as false and slanderous, and especially affirming with peculiar earnestness that the recent act of violence [the murder of Uncle Jerry] which had startled and amazed this law-abiding community was not the work of any of its citizens, but an irruption from beyond its borders.[64]

At this meeting Southerners "turned the torrent of their denunciatory wrath upon the Fool, and gave free rein to their fancy as they invented for him a boyhood, youth, and early manhood, sufficiently degraded and infamous to fit him for the career of the carpetbagger."[65] The citizens of his county insist on an open confession by Servosse, and they express an unwillingness to "permit such communications to pass without their notice and condemnation."[66] Servosse defends his letter, claiming that the acts of aggression have been indeed as great as he stated.

His open defiance of Southerners, his unwillingness to suppress his unceasing advocacy of the Negro, his sharp censure of these extremists who have abused the scalawag Jesse Hyman and the Negro Bob and who have murdered John Walters and Uncle Jerry lead inevitably to the climax of the novel—the personal confrontation of Servosse's daughter with the Ku Klux Klan. While Servosse is accompanying Judge Denton, a fellow abolitionist and a despised scalawag, to his home, his daughter Lily receives an anonymous note stating that Denton and her father are in danger of being attacked by the Klan. Tourgée presents his heroine as courageous and indefatigable; Lily, like 'Toinette in *A Royal Gentleman*, like the typical heroine of Reconstruction fiction, is sentimentally eulogized. So committed was Tourgée to the standard conception of woman's nobility and purity that he did not attempt to differentiate between the qualities of Northern and Southern women.

The scene is related in the usual melodramatic manner of flight and pursuit; yet Tourgée's description of her attempt to save her father is the most compelling in the book. It is a frenetic scene, thrust in a novel too often retarded by verbose disquisitions on the problems of Reconstruction. The scene, based on an actual experience of Tourgée,[67] illuminates all of Tourgée's arguments; and, though the literary terms in which they are stated prove to be as maudlin as those of most sentimental fiction, the subject matter—the capitulation of the Ku Klux Klan—redeems the excessive sentimentality.

The inner workings and the power of the Ku Klux Klan are described in forceful terms when one of its loyal members, John Burleson, becomes disenchanted by the cruelty of the organization. "We are advancing the power of a party to which we are devoted, it is true [Burleson warns a fellow Ku Kluxer]; but in so doing we are merely putting power in the hands of its worst elements, against whom we shall have to rebel sooner or later. The leaders in these cowardly raids . . . will be our representatives, senators, legislators, judges, and so forth, here-after. . . . When it comes to preferring midnight murderers and brutal assassins for legislators and governors and judges, and the like, simply *because* they were leaders in crime . . . it comes hard! Some time or other we shall be sick and ashamed of it."[68]

Burleson, who openly defies the brotherhood, reveals to Servosse and Judge Denton the names of its members. Frightened by such confessions, other Ku Kluxers acknowledge murders in which they have been involved; as a consequence, the whole Empire crumbles internally. "So the Ku-Klux was buried," Servosse concludes, "and such is the influence of peace and good-will, when united with amnesty and pardon, that in a twelve-month it was forgotten, and he who chanced to refer to so old and exploded a joke was greeted with the laughter-provoking cry of the 'bloody shirt.' "[69]

But Servosse is convinced that the abandonment of the Klan

does not mean that Southern white supremacy is extinct; he realizes that it will merely assume different forms. The inflexible resistance of Southern pride causes him to consider his personal venture a failure; for he has learned that the spirit, the mode of thought, the life of the North, cannot be imposed upon the South. "We presumed," he states at the end of the novel, "that, by the suppression of rebellion, the Southern white man had become identical with the Caucasian of the North in thought and sentiment; and that the slave, by emancipation, had become a saint and a Solomon at once. So we tried to build up communities there which would be identical in thought, sentiment, growth and development, with those of the North. It was a FOOL'S ERRAND."[70]

Tourgée's novel ends abruptly and unrealistically. The last truly dramatic scene is Lily Servosse's "race against time"; but after this lengthy description, which, though melodramatic, is effective because of its integral relationship with the reign of terror that dominates the central section of the novel, Tourgée retreats into the sentimental denouement that marks the conclusion of so many novels of Reconstruction. Melville Gurney, who is a "royal gentleman," a typical Southern hero, wishes to marry Lily Servosse but his parents object, "not so much because" the Servosses "are Northerners as because they are *not* Southerners—are strangers so to speak; not of *us*, nor imbued with our feelings; speaking our language, but not thinking our thoughts."[71] Eventually Gurney's father reluctantly acquiesces to the marriage, never completely accepting Lily Servosse but admitting that "she's just the girl I'd like Melville to marry, if she wasn't a Yankee, and her daddy wasn't a Radical."[72] This sentimental relationship, so artificially and arbitrarily introduced in the novel, is an inversion of the usual reconciliation motive to be found in most of the fiction of Reconstruction—here the Southerner grows to recognize the noble qualities of the Republican, even though he cannot accept his politics. But the love affair is extraneous to any real importance the novel has—it is merely Tourgée's automatic gesture to the popular fiction of the period, his appeal to the average reader of both the North and the South.

The last years of Servosse's life in North Carolina are not mentioned by Tourgée; and, unlike his own experiences, which were characterized by a sharp decline of political and social importance, they are filled with Servosse's glorified activities for "a company of capitalists" in Central America. The novel concludes with Servosse's perceptive insights into the failure of Reconstruction, but it does not indicate how Servosse was affected—as Tourgée and all Republicans were radically affected —by the change in the political power of the South. This kind of omission, which really amounts to distortion here and elsewhere in the novel, is the chief defect of *A Fool's Errand*; and it indicates again why the reader must be particularly careful before he accepts the novel as autobiographical—Tourgée was too personally involved, too self-consciously defensive, in recalling his own experiences to be honest about their less attractive features.

Servosse dies as a consequence of yellow fever contracted on his travels in Central America. His unexpected illness elicits a warm response on the part of Southerners who spontaneously volunteer to nurse him, and his death is mourned by all the people who knew him during his residence in the South. Tourgée quotes as a typical Southern reaction to Servosse's death—in actuality to his own career in the South—the following statement from the *Verdenton Gazette*:

> Colonel Servosse removed to this country from the State of Michigan immediately after the war, and has resided here constantly until about a year since. He was an active and able political leader, and was instrumental in molding and shaping legislation under the Reconstruction measures to a very great extent. Naturally, he was the mark for very bitter political attack, and was for a time, no doubt, greatly misrepresented. That he was a man of marked ability is now universally admitted, and it is generally conceded that he was thoroughly honest in the views which he entertained. Personally, he was a man of fine qualities, who made many and fast friends. He is not thought to have been capable of deliberate and persistent malice; but his audacious and unsparing ridicule of the men and measures he opposed prevented many of his opponents from appreciating the other valuable and attractive elements of his character. Whatever may have been their past relations, however, our citizens will be sincerely sorry to learn of his death.[73]

This self-appraisal may seem excessively laudatory, but in reality it is an almost literal transcription of some of the comments Southerners made upon Tourgée's own departure from

North Carolina and at his death. A Southern journalist, writing Tourgée's obituary in 1905, correctly characterized him as a judge who "was personally held in high esteem in the community where his politics were contemned by every white man of Southern birth. In that section where he presided as magistrate of an alien court, to judge of the transactions of a proud and brave people, he was held in great esteem because of his virtues and ability."[74] And in 1944, William A. Devin expressed the opinion that most modern historians of North Carolina have of Tourgée: "He left the imprint of his mind and thought upon the constitution and laws of the state which neither time nor change has eradicated. While he was unloved in North Carolina, he won from those who disagreed with him respect for his legal learning and judicial capacity, and admiration for the courage with which he championed the cause of those whose rights he thought were denied."[75]

But the true conclusion of *A Fool's Errand* is not Servosse's death, which proves to be a convenient and arbitrary way to terminate a hero's career that otherwise would have to become decidedly anticlimactic; the novel really closes on Servosse's suggestion for a solution to the manifold problems of Reconstruction—national education. In terms of Tourgée's novel, this is a fitting conclusion, for we are convinced that Servosse has honestly erred in his humanitarian approach to the complex political issues which confronted him, and that now he is qualified to arrive at a sober and intelligent opinion. We believe in the significance of his personal failure and in the validity of his considered answer to the besetting question of what the nation must do with the newly freed Negro. Comfort Servosse, failing to comfort and serve the colored man immediately, serves him by transcending that personal defeat, by insisting upon one answer—primary education.

Servosse's advocacy of education in 1871 is indeed sensible and admirable, and artistically plausible; we respect him for his moderate proposals as an intelligent Northerner. But we must remember that Tourgée himself did not arrive at these conclusions until 1877, when he began to write *A Fool's Errand*; throughout his own residence in North Carolina he did not admit defeat until Radical Republicanism had failed. Now, with the publication of *A Fool's Errand* and his other Reconstruction novels, he sought to reopen old wounds, and he sought to arouse

Northern interest in Southern problems. In doing so, he motivated
his heroes as he himself would have preferred to be motivated.

Realizing that practical proposals which oppose the Southerner's cherished and well-established customs will not raise the
Negro to a position of equality, Tourgée's hero turns to the
panacea of the idealist—education. Ignorance, he feels, has
made the Negro afraid of the Ku Klux Klan; ignorance has made
the Southerner fear the freed and aspiring Negro; ignorance has
shut the Northern mind to the deep-seated issues of Reconstruction; and ignorance has caused carpetbaggers like Servosse to
act impetuously and inconsiderately. Throughout his novel,
Tourgée berates the government for having failed to support
him and other Republicans when they were challenging the
supremacy of the Ku Klux Klan. "It was difficult," as Edmund
Wilson suggests, "for the Northerners to realize that the Southerners were not definitely squelched. They never, in fact, really
learned the truth till the appearance of *A Fool's Errand* in 1879,
and then they made haste to forget it."[76] In a chapter entitled
"Wisdom and Folly Meet Together," Tourgée insists that the
federal government must assume the responsibility of educating
all illiterates of the South:

> Let the Nation educate the colored man and the poor-white
> *because* the Nation held them in bondage, and is responsible for
> their education; educate the voter *because* the Nation cannot
> afford that he should be ignorant. Do not try to shuffle off the
> responsibility, nor cloak the danger. Honest ignorance in the
> masses is more to be dreaded than malevolent intelligence in
> the few. It furnished the rank and file of rebellion and the
> prejudice-minded multitudes who made the Policy of Repression
> effectual. Poor-whites, Freedmen, Ku Klux, and Bulldozers are
> all alike the harvest of ignorance. The Nation cannot afford to
> grow such a crop.[77]

The value of *A Fool's Errand* lies in Tourgée's report of the
political failure of Radical Republicanism during Reconstruction.
Though we are fully conscious of Tourgée's bias in writing
A Fool's Errand, though we know that he has presented his
Northern carpetbagger as the selfless reformer that his prototype
and author was not, we are also aware that he is able to appreciate and dramatize some of the major reasons for the failure
of Radical Republicanism in the South. We also realize that we

are confronted with a significant and rare interpretation of Reconstruction by a Northerner, one with cogent insights expressed in a forceful and emotionally persuasive language. Nevertheless, the novel is full of omissions: Tourgée ignores the misappropriation of public funds for which the Republicans were largely responsible; he never mentions Holden's use of the militia to suppress the Ku Klux Klan; and he fails to record the growth of the Union League—the one organization most immediately responsible for the Ku Klux Klan in North Carolina. His report is, after all, a rationalization of the Republican's attempt to reconstruct the "poor, misguided and mismanaged South."[78]

Tourgée's novel also suffers from the usual limitations of most sentimental fiction: a factitious romance between the Southern gentleman and the Northern girl, incredible coincidences, excessive dissertations on the morality and proper conduct of Servosse, murders and attempted murders, the unassailable loyalty of Servosse's wife, the melodramatic intrepidity of his daughter. Though he was engaged in describing events whose actuality demanded a realistic treatment, Tourgée felt a stronger commitment to the long tradition of sentimental literature that preceded his own writings. While he was able to render the brutality of the Ku Klux Klan in what he considered truthful terms, he could not be so realistic in his description of human relations. The reconciliation motive is used as the artificial resolution of his novel: the Northern heroine effects the conversion of her Southern lover.

But in A Fool's Errand—and this is not true of the other literature of Reconstruction—the history and eventual demise of Radical Republicanism is viewed sympathetically; the carpetbagger regime is considered as a failure—a failure whose responsibility is that of the national government—but it is not described as only a political system of opportunists. Though Tourgée was at first as biased from his point of view as Thomas Nelson Page and Thomas Dixon were from theirs, he was astute enough to recognize the misguided and ill-timed humanitarianism of many carpetbaggers; and he showed a growing sympathy for Southerners that was rare for a Republican who had been so passionately radical in his early political career.

Tourgée's foolish errand is that he tried to enforce against horrendous odds the impracticable Reconstruction policies of the Federal government. His anger—and anger is the dominant mood in this bitter book—is finally directed not, as we might suspect, at Southerners, but at the inept, "wise" politicians of the North who have betrayed the Negro, the poor white, and even the impoverished Southern planter. Edmund Wilson is certainly justified in asserting that Tourgée "came to understand the Southerner's point of view, not merely from firsthand observation but with a sympathetic intuition such as, so far as I know, was exercised by no other Northern invader who has put himself on record, and this makes him a unique witness whose work is an invaluable source."[79] In *A Fool's Errand* the "folly" of Radical Republicanism takes on a credibility which exists in none of the other Reconstruction fiction, because the Republican is human.

III *Critical and Popular Reception*

The popularity of *A Fool's Errand* was extraordinary, for Tourgée had written a tale that not only carried historical import for his reading public but was the first extended fictional commentary on Reconstruction. And Northerners, who had been exposed only to journalistic accounts, were eager to read the personal interpretation of a defeated carpetbagger. The New York *Tribune*, a Republican newspaper, enthusiastically endorsed the novel: "Few works of the day have had a more rapid and immediate success than 'A Fool's Errand' now enjoys. No book on our shop counters sells better and the fame of it has been carried on the wings of newspapers into every State if not county in the land. Its reception in the South has not been of the most cordial kind though the merit of it as a composition is not denied."[80]

This was indeed true, for as *The Raleigh Observer* admitted, the story "is a powerfully written work, and destined, we fear, to do as much harm in the world as 'Uncle Tom's Cabin,' to which it is, indeed, a companion piece."[81] Cornelia Phillips Spencer, who lived near Tourgée during Reconstruction, praised the novel highly: "I have just read Tourgée's *Fool's Errand*," she wrote in her diary. "It is very smart, and the only book on this phase of the South and North that presents a true picture. He has done it very well. Tells the truth as nearly as a Carpetbagger and a Tourgée could be expected to do. I think he tried to be fair."[82] *Harper's Magazine* offered perhaps the most tempered and just commentary on the quality of the book: "It can scarcely be called a love story. . . . It is rather an earnest and at times passionate philippic in narrative form against the reconstruction policy . . . The volume is one sided, but intensely earnest."[83]

Later critics were to find the novel one of the most illuminating analyses of Reconstruction problems in American literature, though they did not qualify their remarks with the observation that it was also one of the few fictional interpretations—and not merely descriptions—of the period. C. Alphonso Smith, the biographer of O. Henry, commented: "After reading many special treatises and university dissertations on the kind of Reconstruction attempted in the South I find in 'A Fool's Errand' the wisest statement of the whole question yet made."[84]

In addition to the popular material Tourgée included in his book, the title of the novel helped to aid its attraction, for it read *A Fool's Errand by One of the Fools.* This riddle led to much conjecture on the part of the critics; and individuals as different as the governor of South Carolina, General Ames of Mississippi, General Joseph Abbott, Harriet Beecher Stowe, and Tourgée himself were suggested as the possible author. Tourgée was aware that the riddle might increase the sales of the book: "The writer believed that the form of the title would constitute one of those pleasant literary conundrums which have a distinct market value, and would consequently enhance the sale of the book."[85] So great was the reception of the book, in fact, that, including editions that were offered to the public in the same volume with *The Invisible Empire,* almost two hundred thousand copies were sold.[86]

The popularity of the novel and the success that an unauthorized dramatization had enjoyed in the West caused Tourgée to collaborate with the playwright Steele MacKaye in the writing of an authorized version. MacKaye revised Tourgée's written version and thereafter handled the structural details of the play. Tourgée supplied the information and verified the facts. But the play closed two weeks after its opening in October, 1881, in Philadelphia.

The novel evoked a great response from various dissident readers. In January, 1881, appeared William Royall's *A Reply to A Fool's Errand by One of the Fools,* presenting a carefully documented refutation of Tourgée's novel. Royall states his aims in his preface: "I look upon the book to which I have attempted to reply as a willful and malicious libel upon a noble and generous people. . . . I look upon its author as one of the most contemptible fellows of those who have libeled that people, and not at all less contemptible because highly endowed with intellect."[87] Royall proceeds to accuse Tourgée of not recording the Negro dialect faithfully, and he refuses to accept Tourgée's notion that most Southerners hated the North as much as they hated the Negro. He further maintains that the barren state of the South was largely due to carpetbaggers; Tourgée, in the New York *Tribune,* offered a lengthy rebuttal. Royall, a Southerner by birth, produces little convincing evidence in his denunciation of Tourgée's analysis of Reconstruction problems; and, as the New York *Tribune* maintained, was "satisfied with pronouncing the statements of Judge Tourgée as 'false as hell'—a mode of reasoning which can hardly be called conclusive."[88] Royall's prejudices were even greater than those of Tourgée.

The Reverend J. H. Ingraham, in his collection of letters entitled *Not A Fool's Errand,* also attempts to reveal Tourgée's wrong-headed approach to Southern conditions. His heroine, a Northern governess, goes to the South, is converted to the Southern way of living, and so considers her journey "not a fool's errand."

Ingraham's book was an ineffective retort to *A Fool's Errand,* as was Harriet Goff's *Other Fools and Their Doings,* where the injuries that landowners inflicted on freedmen are dramatized. More elaborate than any of these rebuttals, however, was N. J. Floyd's *Thorns in the Flesh.* Floyd confessed to be "a layman in the field of literature,"[89] but he considered it his duty as a Southerner to answer Tourgée's novel: "The South has been virtually silent for twenty years respecting the slanders that have been and are being heaped upon her by every type of the radical Puritan notoriety, from him who writes himself a Fool with a capital 'F' down to the less ambitious and less egotistical creatures who are content to wait for an intelligent public to apply that appropriate epithet, and to spell it with a lower case initial letter."[90]

The first half of Floyd's political tract is a defense of slavery. Towards the end of his verbose, diffuse book, he directly attacks those "knaves errant" who shared in the "carnivals of rapine and villainy in the prostrate, suffering South" and who wrote anti-Southern novels.[91] In meticulous fashion he attempts to refute Tourgée's major arguments, particularly those in support of the Negro and in condemnation of the Ku Klux Klan. But Floyd is so chauvinistic that the reader can anticipate his every argument. Once again we are confronted with a typical, and not very meritorious, defense of the South: "We [the Southern people] possess," Floyd writes, "a higher civilization—North, as well as South—than was ever known to any people who engaged in civil strife on a large scale."[92]

And when his book was published in 1884, the Southern press hailed the author as a worthy opponent to Harriet Beecher Stowe and Tourgée: "We know the author to be a fine writer, and his views are not only sound, but conservative, and still they are Southern and Virginian through and through. We have needed such a book . . . Judge Tourgée has given us since the war what Miss Stowe did before, and we have suffered for the want of a popular book vindicating our side of a controversy that looks as if it started at Plymouth Rock and will stop only at the North Pole."[93]

None of these works succeeded in preventing *A Fool's Errand* from becoming extremely popular; in fact, they helped its sales by forming a controversy over the issues Tourgée considered. One of the most widely read novels in the first year of its publication, it provided Tourgée with more money than he was ever to have again. Yet, despite the success of the novel, he did not want to write of the South again; he sensed that any new political novel of his might be merely a pale reproduction of *A Fool's Errand.* He was doubtless correct, but he found himself with the common problem that faces all commercially successful novelists: having achieved his popularity by treating of Southern conditions, he was urged by his publishers to consider the same issues in another novel. Tourgée finally acquiesced; within a short time *Bricks Without Straw* appeared.

CHAPTER 5

Bricks Without Straw: The Negro
in Reconstruction Literature

TOURGÉE, in *Bricks Without Straw*, offers his most graphic and detailed description of the status of the Negro in the South. His objective in *A Fool's Errand* was comprehensive: he confronted a humanitarian of the North with the South's hostility and revealed the humanitarian's slow understanding and appreciation of the intricate problems of Reconstruction. In *Bricks Without Straw*, Tourgée focuses his attention on the Negro and succeeds in developing a better structured plot than he was able to create in any of his other novels, with the possible exception of *Murvale Eastman*. Whereas in *A Fool's Errand* the Negro was described as the "wretched freedman," as a man molested by the Ku Klux Klan and powerless before its domination, we now see him as an active outcast, as an ambitious and insurgent freedman who will not complacently wait for the white man to accord him, in his daily life, rights that he legally possesses. The colored people, an educated and self-sufficient Negro observes, "can only be made free by knowledge. I begin to see that the law can only give us the opportunity to make ourselves freemen. Liberty must be earned; it cannot be given."[1]

I   *The Negro*

Tourgée's view of the Negro stands in sharp contrast to that of almost all the other important writers of Reconstruction. The singularity of his position can scarcely be appreciated unless we are aware of how other authors, dealing with the same material, treat the central issue of all Reconstruction fiction: the economic and social equality of the Negro. Whereas the hero of the literature is the "gentleman," the victim is the Negro; and his presence, like that of the gentleman, is felt everywhere in post-bellum writing. Before we examine *Bricks Without Straw* closely, we ought to observe the treatment that authors like Thomas Nelson Page, Joel Chandler Harris, and Thomas Dixon have given to the Negro so as to see more clearly the literary and cultural context within which Tourgée is writing. By the early 1880's, the time during which *Bricks Without Straw* appeared, Southern writers had so succeeded in dominating the American literary scene that even Tourgée admitted that they had achieved a victory: "Our literature has become not only Southern in type, but distinctly Confederate in sympathy. . . . A foreigner studying our current literature, without knowledge of our history and judging our civilization by our fiction, would undoubtedly conclude that the South was the seat of intellectual empire in America, and the African the chief romantic element of our population."[2]

From the point of view of most Southern authors, the Negro was villain or saint—depending on whether or not he actively asserted his rights as freedman. If he demanded equal opportunity as a newly enfranchised citizen, he was pictured as partner in the Republican conspiracy to undermine the congenial race relations that had existed in ante-bellum times; if, on the other hand, he desired to perpetuate his role as servant, he was drawn as a contented Negro who enjoyed status in Southern society, gained the admiration of his kindly masters, and in turn recognized the natural and proper supremacy of the white man. As Tourgée observed, there were two types of Negroes: "the devoted slave, happy if the scene was laid in days of slavery, the guardian of his white folks if the grimmer postwar South was the period of the story, and the confused freedman who usually was rescued from semi-ludicrous predicaments by the white people to whom he once had belonged."[3]

In the fiction of Thomas Nelson Page and of Thomas Dixon this condescending attitude toward the Negro is most obvious; but it also appears in the stories and novels of Joel Chandler Harris, Mary Murfree, Maurice Thompson, and innumerable minor writers. Harris seemed to be able to share the fears and laughter and anger of the Negro; and he contributed the most popular Negro characters to American fiction—Uncle Remus,

Balaam, Ananias, and Mingo. But when he wrote his own Reconstruction novel, *Gabriel Tolliver*, in 1902, Harris could not completely sympathize with the Negro who had insisted on immediate reconstruction. The average Negroes—the illiterate colored men who blindly supported the Union League—he depicted as misguided children controlled by Republicans; for them, Harris had only a feeling of compassion. "The niggers ain't no more to blame for all this trouble than a parcel of two-year-old children," a Southerner comments. "You mark my words: the niggers will suffer, and these white rascals will go scot free."[4] But, for the colored leader who supported the Union League, Harris felt only hatred; he was certain that he was using his fellow Negroes for his own aggrandizement:

> He [the Reverend Jeremiah, leader of the Negroes] was not a vicious Negro. In common with the great majority of his race—in common, perhaps with the men of all races—he was eaten up by a desire to become prominent, to make himself conspicuous. Generations of civilization (as it is called) have gone far to control it to some extent, though now and then we see it crop out in individuals. But there had been no toning down of the Reverent Jeremiah's egotism; on the contrary, it had been fed on the flattery of his congregation until it was gross and rank.[5]

Reconstruction, from Harris' viewpoint, was a tragedy for all participants. The final catastrophe of *Gabriel Tolliver* is a result of the immoral manipulation of Negroes: a colored man, who has been urged against his will to join the Radicals, murders the white Republican leader of the Union League because he believes erroneously that the carpetbagger is having an affair with his mulatto wife. The Republican is a pious, ascetic man, fanatically dedicated to a futile cause; the mulatto wife feels vaguely superior to her pure-bred Negro husband and attempts to seduce the carpetbagger; and the Negro, the most lamentable figure in the book, is an uncertain, confused man. Having forsaken the Southern white master whom he was able to trust, he is taught to desire luxuries that have never been a part of his culture. Harris does not censure the common Negro for his actions during Reconstruction; whatever anger is in his book—and there is comparatively little—is directed toward those Northerners who insisted on "Americanizing" the Southerner.

Harris primarily described the comic and the local-color Negro, although, in writing of Reconstruction, he saw the colored man as wretched and bewildered. Thomas Nelson Page also saw the comic aspects of the Negro; but he, more than any other writer, fostered the image of the contented slave. His best stories— "Marse Chan," "Meh Lady," and "Ole 'Stracted"—recall the allegedly congenial race relations which existed "befoah the war," when, from the point of view of the Negro, "dyar warn' no trouble nor nuthin'."[6] Thus Page expressed the legend of a past splendor through the ex-slaves themselves, "those upon whose labor the system was founded and for whose sake it was destroyed."[7]

In all of Page's writings there is an implicit racist note. This bias becomes particularly conspicuous whenever Page defends "The Old South" after the war: "In art, in mechanical development, in literature, in mental and moral science, in all the range of mental action, no notable work has up to this time come from a negro. . . . The leopard cannot change his spots today nor the Ethiopian his skin, any more than they could in the days of Jeremiah, the son of Halkiah. . . . Where the negro has thriven it has invariably been under the influence and by the assistance of the stronger race."[8]

Although Page supported the restored Union, he felt that the only healthy solution to the race problem would stem from the master-slave relationship which existed before the Civil War. The Negro needed guidance, Page knew; but he asserted repeatedly that the guidance should be given by the Southerner —the Negro problem, after all, was a Southern problem. And the late nineteenth-century Northern legislators, as Rayford W. Logan has pointed out, tended to agree with him.[9]

In his two Reconstruction novels, *Red Rock* (1898) and *The Red Riders* (1924), Page was compelled because of his bias to picture the "Wretched" or "Brute Negro." The real villains, as in Harris' *Gabriel Tolliver,* are the carpetbaggers and scalawags; but Page could not be so sympathetic as Harris toward those Negroes who had deserted their masters and now misused their newly won rights. They idly hovered about railway stations, he noted; they were discourteous to the white gentry—to those who had been only benevolent and considerate in ante-bellum times; and they supported the most abhorrent Republican leaders. Page heightened his characterization by contrasting these "unfaithful" Negroes with the few loyal freedmen who refused to leave the plantation. "I was born 'pon dis plantation," remarks one devoted Negro, "and I has lived here de length of man's allotted days, an' I seed three ginerations come and go right here, and I has always considered it my home and I still considers it so."[10]

Page could not understand the freedman—he could not appreciate the difficulties which confronted the Negro because of emancipation. As one Negro critic, Sterling Brown, has pointed out, Page presents a distorted picture of what freedom meant to the Negro:

> Slavery was to be shown as not slavery at all, but a happy state best suited for an inferior, childish but lovable race. In this normal condition, the Negro was shown as thriving. Then came his emancipation, which the better class of Negroes did not want, and which few could understand or profit by. Freedom meant anarchy. Only by restoring control (euphemism for tenant farming, sharecropping, black codes, enforced labor, segregation and all the other ills of the new slavery) could equilibrium in the South, so important to the nation be achieved.[11]

Because of Page's narrow point of view, *Red Rock* (1898) and *The Red Riders* (1924) fail as novels. All the characters are stereotypes, as their names clearly suggest: Jonadab Leech, the carpetbagger; Joseph Grease, the scalawag; Captain Middleton, a respected Northern commander of Virginia. Characters are not defined as human beings; they are used as propaganda instruments—in spite of the fact that Page struggled to avoid creating political tracts. In a letter to Arthur Hobson Quinn, he referred to his difficulties in writing *Red Rock*:

> It may interest you to know that when I first undertook to write "Red Rock," after having written a third or more of the novel I discovered that I had drifted into the production of a political tract. I bodily discarded what I had written, and going back beyond the War, in order to secure a background and a point of departure which would enable me to take a more serene path, I rewrote it entirely. I had discovered that the real facts in the Reconstruction period were so terrible that I was unable to describe them fully. The story of this period of National madness will doubtless be written some time and if any man will steep himself as I did, myself, in such records as the "Ku Klux Reports" issued by the Government in 1872, and, "A Voice from South

Carolina" published in Charleston by Dr. Leland in 1879; "The Prostrate State," and the newspapers of the reconstruction period I think he will agree with me in feeling that we are too near the time to be able to present the facts with true art.[12]

Unlike Tourgée, Page did not witness the Reconstruction period as an adult; in 1867 he was only fourteen years of age. It seems clear, therefore, that his "sources," in addition to newspapers, were his memories of adult talk. *The Prostrate State*, the Ku Klux Reports, and John A. Leland's *A Voice from South Carolina* merely served to reinforce the bias he had acquired in his youth. And yet, despite the sensitive Southern pride which colors *Red Rock* and *The Red Riders,* despite the distortions which result from Page's bias, it should be noted that *Red Rock* was the first account of Reconstruction which was frankly rendered; Page felt no inhibitions in writing his novel.

The Southern authors' characterization of the Negro proved to be immensely popular. In the 1880's such Northern writers as Frank Stockton, Harriet Spofford, and Constance Fenimore Woolson accepted the Southern version of Reconstruction; the admirable freedman of Reconstruction was the devoted Negro who recalled his contented existence before the war and who voluntarily remained faithful to his past masters.[13] As Tourgée realized, the favorite formula of Reconstruction authors— Northern and Southern—was one in which the Negro alleviated his ex-master's poverty. In Harris' "Aunt Fountain's Prisoner" the Negro divided with the whites the rations he received from the Freedman's Bureau; in Jeannie Woodville's "Uncle Pompey's Christmas" he stole for his former owners; in Octave Thanet's *Half-a-Curse* (1887) he supported his previous master by fighting a rapacious overseer. At times he maintained a pride in the disintegrating manor house, as in Virginia Boyle's *Brockenburne* (1897), Frances Baylor's *Claudia Hyde* (1894), and Paul Dunbar's "The Colonel's Awakening" (1898). Or, if he had been affected by the new radical ideas of the Republicans, he experimented with freedom—as in Harris' "Mom-Bi" (1887) and Mrs. Boyle's "A Kingdom for Micajah" (1900)—but he quickly returned to the contented existence of the slave. More often, however, the noble Negro—like Aunt Martha of William Baker's *Mose Evans* (1874)—refused to attempt freedom under any conditions. If we were to judge the prewar status of the Negro from the fiction of these authors, we would be convinced that the colored man enjoyed rare security in ante-bellum times.[14]

These Reconstruction novels and stories were a lament for a tradition authors felt was being undermined; the authors' condemnation of the freedman was largely reinforced by the reminder of better days before the war. Reconstruction writers were rarely bitter; indeed they can be considered only mild racists when their works are compared with those of Thomas Dixon, Jr., the most reactionary apologist of slavery and the Ku Klux Klan. Dixon employed many of the same characters, institutions, and situations as Page and other Southern authors; indeed Reconstruction writers had helped to prepare the reading public for Dixon's novels by recalling the healthy conditions before the war and endorsing, if only mildly, a caste system in the post-bellum South.

Dixon made no attempt to conceal either his anti-Negro bias or his staunch defense of an Aryan civilization in America. His novels were extremely popular, for they were published at a time when race relations had deteriorated in the South and "the extremists of Southern racism [had] probably reached a wider audience, both within their own region and in the nation, than ever before. . . . It was a time when the hope born of Reconstruction had all but died for the Negro, when disfranchisement blocked his political advance and the caste system closed the door to integration in the white world, when the North had abandoned him to the South and the South was yielding to the clamor of her extremists."[15]

Dixon wrote what he described as "The Trilogy of Reconstruction," but in actuality his three novels—*The Leopard's Spots* (1902), *The Clansman* (1905), and *The Traitor* (1907)—are a chronicle and a defense of the Ku Klux Klan. In *The Leopard's Spots*, the hero, a preacher, bemoans the fact that Negro dominion, deification, "equality and amalgamation" have been forced upon Southerners against their will.[16] The Ku Klux Klan, he maintains, "was simply the old answer of organized manhood to organized crime. Its purpose was to bring order out of chaos, protect the weak and defenceless, the widows and orphans of brave men who had died for their country, to drive from power the thieves who were robbing the people, redeem the commonwealth from infamy, and re-establish civilisation."[17]

Dixon describes the Reconstruction policies of the Republicans

as an "attempt to establish with the bayonet an African barbarism on the ruins of Southern society," and he characterized
such an attempt as "a conspiracy against human progress. It
was the blackest crime of the nineteenth century."[18] The violent
crimes of the Negro are delineated in detail; so antagonistic are
the freedmen to their former masters, in fact, that the birth
of the Ku Klux Klan is almost justified. The organization is led
by a moderate Southerner and not a fanatic—Dixon models
his hero after his own uncle, Colonel Leroy McAfee, who was
actually Grand Titan of the Invisible Empire; and it is clearly
indicated that the Klan is formed only as a defense of Southern
rights. When the Republicans and Negroes have been completely
overwhelmed by the Klan, its leader announces that he has been
"a successful revolutionist—that Civilization has been saved,
and the South redeemed from shame."[19]

Thomas Dixon was far more reactionary than most Southern
writers. His novels appeared in the first decade of the twentieth
century, and by that time Reconstruction, the Ku Klux Klan,
and the Union League were as historical to Northerners as the
subject matter of *Uncle Tom's Cabin* was to Southerners; the
Ku Klux Klan, of course, was revived later in the century.[20]
Few authors of the South shared Dixon's attitudes, and the
lasting portrait of the Negro remained that of Joel Chandler
Harris and Thomas Nelson Page. Nevertheless, Dixon's novels
do recapture the feelings of many Southerners during Reconstruction, and they evoked an overwhelmingly favorable reaction
when presented as dramas throughout the South.[21]

From Tourgée, however, Dixon's novels evoked only violent
protest. When asked by a reviewer to comment on *The Leopard's
Spots* (1902), Tourgée wrote a lengthy "personal and con-
fidential" letter, denouncing Dixon's version of Reconstruction:

> The book is entirely worthless as a narrative of events or an
> analysis of causes. It bears not the remotest similitude to any-
> thing that ever happened. As a picture of the times, it is not
> worth discussion, but as a delineation of the southern white man
> of yesterday and to-day, it is of inestimable value. I have known
> Dixon almost from his boyhood . . . know his type and the
> influences by which he and those like him have been shaped.
> There are many admirable things about these people. But their
> view of events is colored wholly by the prejudices of the class
> and section and their ideal of God is simply a being endowed

with the impulses and sentiments of the southern white man. . . .

This is what Dixon's book teaches and luminously shows to be the dominating impulse of the southern whites of the best class—of the perfect, inerrant, impeccable type. Anhilation [*sic*], deportation or eternal and unresisting subjection to the will and pleasure of the white people.—These are the only alternatives which a Christian minister offers to the colored people of the U. S.![22]

The Negroes in Tourgée's fiction are outcasts, independent people who refuse to resume their abject role of slave and are consequently denied full freedom by the whites. 'Toinette, the mulatto heroine of *A Royal Gentleman,* has been educated by her white lover, but once the war is over she demands equal rights; Tourgée carefully informs us that 'Toinette has been emancipated intellectually as well as legally. Nimbus, the Negro protagonist of *Bricks Without Straw,* insists on the opportunity to earn his livelihood, to improve his economic status; but, when he begins to prosper, the white community suppresses him, and he is forced to escape to the North.

Tourgée's portrait of the Negro is, of course, not wholly accurate. Since his knowledge of ante-bellum conditions was academic rather than personal, he knew little of the Negro as slave. Moreover, he refused to admit that the freedman of Reconstruction, for whatever extenuating reasons one might mention, did steal and at times murder; many of the post-bellum Negroes felt that slavery "had won for them the right to refrain from work, to live in idleness and enjoy themselves."[23] In Tourgée's fiction the Negro is hero; he is never viewed as unruly or insurgent. His former master becomes the villain. The portrait of the South during Reconstruction which Harris and Page drew is now reversed; and Tourgée, in attempting to explore the Negro character, errs in the opposite direction: the independent freedman, described as a menace to a white Southern civilization in the literature of Southern authors, is idealized by Tourgée.

Tourgée rebelled against the stereotyped portrait of the Negro that appeared in post-bellum fiction. Part of his rebellion was naturally caused by his political bias—all of these authors wrote with a conviction in Negro inferiority. But Tourgée was also convinced that even from the point of view of literature, the American writer was not appreciating the potentialities of the Negro as a fictional character.

About the Negro as a man [he wrote in 1888] with hopes, fears, and aspirations like any other man, our literature is very nearly silent. . . . The Negro is either the devoted slave, but such a man was a miracle—or he is the man to whom liberty has brought only misfortune. Much has been written of the slave and something of the freedman, but thus far no-one has been found able to weld the new life to the old. . . . The life of the Negro as a slave, freedman, and racial outcast offers undoubtedly the richest mine of romantic material that has opened to the English-speaking novelist since the Wizard of the North discovered and depicted the common life of Scotland. The Negro as a man has an immense advantage over the Negro as servant, being an altogether new character in fiction.[24]

Tourgée's literary theory was more accurate than his practice. The Negro as an outcast did offer vast possibilities to late nineteenth-century authors, though few of them—Mark Twain is a notable exception—took full advantage of the new fictional character. Tourgée himself saw the freedman too narrowly, and it was not until the twentieth century that authors were able to describe the Negro as someone not always being manipulated for political purposes.

II Theory of Progress

The history of Nimbus, the central figure of *Bricks Without Straw*, is traced from his birth until the time the Ku Klux Klan terrorizes him and his family so much that he is forced to leave the South. Nimbus is Tourgée's archetypal Negro: he is uneducated but intelligent, kind but firm in his demands for freedom, and the protector of those weaker mortals of his own race. Nimbus represents to Tourgée the latent spirit in the Negro that now, in its first moments of birth, awkwardly strives for selfhood. Indeed, so truculent is Tourgée's protagonist in his fierce demands for equal rights that he often appears excessively, unattractively aggressive. To condone Nimbus' actions is to share unqualifiedly Tourgée's bias, for Nimbus insists upon immediate freedom, immediate equality. "I's a free man," he cries, "an' ef I think a man's gran' rascal I'se gwine ter *say* so, whether he's black er white; an' ef enny on 'em comes ter Ku Klux me I'll put a bullet t'rough dem! I will, by God."[25]

The achievement of selfhood for Nimbus is no easy matter.

He must learn a whole new set of values, a whole new attitude toward life—he must learn to be a fundamentally different man. His situation before the Civil War was clear: he was black and therefore inferior; he was inferior and therefore a slave; he was a slave and so did not think. So long as he accepted his situation, no friction existed between him and his master. Not knowing the pains of ambition, he did not suffer for his ignorance. But now, in his new and confusing role as freedman, he finds himself unprepared for such an unprecedented transformation; and he also discovers that his liberators are not to be his teachers.

Nimbus succeeds in raising himself beyond the expectation of those around him. An adventurous man, he and several of his friends buy tobacco lands which prove to be prosperous. In a short time they prove to be too prosperous, for the white community grows wary of this ambitious and self-reliant enemy and virulently censures him: "Our people won't stand a nigger's puttin' on such airs. Why, Captain . . . You just ought to see his place down at Red Wing. Damned if he ain't better fixed than lots of white men in the country. He's got a good house, and one of the finest crops of terbacker in the country. I tell you, he's cutting a wide swath, he is."[26] Through the character of Nimbus, Tourgée offers in *Bricks Without Straw* a practical statement of his theory of progress. Nimbus has all the attributes necessary for material success, but his attempt to rise in the agrarian South is thwarted by envious Southerners. He, as a Negro leader, tries to acquire education and financial stability for himself and his fellow freedmen; but he is frustrated by Southerners who refuse to accept the equality of the Negro.

Yet Nimbus is not without friends. The incorrigibly sentimental Tourgée could not handle a story of any length without introducing his idealized heroine. In *Bricks Without Straw* she is Northerner Mollie Ainslie. Her character need hardly be defined; she is of the same mold as Lily Servosse—audacious, beautiful, independent, athletic, and outspoken.

Mollie Ainslie is a teacher of Negro illiterates; and, like those teachers briefly mentioned in *A Fool's Errand,* she invites the animosity of Southerners by befriending Nimbus and other Negroes. The Northern women who came to the South to teach the Negro were perfect models for fictional heroines. Though they were often tactless in their handling of race relations—as Mollie herself is—their motive in journeying to the South was, from the Northerner's point of view, selfless and noble; and certainly their effect on education was salutary. Primarily responsible for the education of the Negro in the South between 1865 and 1880, most often they were missionaries representing Northern churches. As H. L. Swint has noted, their "outstanding characteristic . . . seems to have been piety."[27]

Yet they were often pawns in the hands of Radical Republicans, and they had little respect for the Southern attitude toward education. In reading Tourgée's *A Fool's Errand* and *Bricks Without Straw*, we are led to believe that all Southerners wanted to impede Negro education. This impression is far from accurate, for,

> in the rural sections of North Carolina there were, in 1866, many schools for Negroes which were taught by Southern white men. . . . Two schools near Fayetville were taught by Southern white men, one of whom was an ex-Confederate soldier. Of seven schools in Cumberland County all except the Fayetville schools were taught by Southern men, one or two by Southern Negroes. These men were working for the sake of pay and not from any philanthropic motives, and their social standing had not suffered in the least because of their occupation.[28]

In reference to Mollie Ainslie of *Bricks Without Straw*, the editors of *The Dial* had an interesting commentary. The Northern women who went to the South, they observed, probably "did not as a usual thing enter on their lonely and perilous task at the childish age of seventeen; and did not invariably become at once the daring riders of glossy steeds, each endowed with the strength of a locomotive, the tricks of a circus mule, and the intelligence, docility, and affectionateness of a sheep-dog. The strength of the book [*Bricks Without Straw*] lies in its true and seeming portraiture of the lower order of characters; its rapid thrillingly graphic narration of incidents both terrible and grotesque; and its tear compelling description of a hapless race of beings."[29]

When the Negroes in *Bricks Without Straw* are forbidden to exercise their vote because they have ostensibly been a social disturbance, Mollie tells the white men that "the worst thing these poor fellows meant to do . . . was to make a parade over their new found privilege—march up to the polls, vote, and march home again."[30] For the moment she is respected and considered an arbiter between the two factions. But enmity grows; and Mollie, condemned for attempting to aid Nimbus and his friends, is finally advised to leave the South: ". . . the white folk own this country, and is going to rule it, and we can't stand no such nigger-equality schools as you are running at Red Wing. It's got to stop, and you'd better pick up and go back North where you come from, and that quick, if you want to keep out of trouble."[31]

Tourgée, who depicts the ravages committed by the Ku Klux Klan as vividly as he did in *A Fool's Errand*, once again indicts the organization for exhibiting the worst traits of a proud people. This attitude of superiority annoyed him—as it did most Northerners—more than any other aspect of the Southern mind, for it was opposed to his deep and unrelenting desire to see all peoples equal. He could not extenuate the actions of the Ku Klux Klan, and in this novel, and more particularly in *The Invisible Empire*, he considered the Klan primarily responsible for the subjugation of the Negro.

The South—Tourgée states repeatedly in *Bricks Without Straw* and in its companion piece, *An Appeal to Caesar*—truly believed in its innate superiority over all other races and peoples. The men believed they were "royal gentlemen," a species of people more stately and impressive, more illustrious and grand, than the North had ever known. The women were ladies, possessing a beauty and charm, a gentility, refinement, and cultivation not to be found elsewhere; for no one else shared their dignity of birth. If one were born Southern, one was deemed superior, for "to praise the South was to praise himself; to boast of its valor was to advertise his own intrepidity; to extol its women was to enhance the glory of his own achievements in the lists of love; to vaunt its chivalry was to avouch his own honor; to laud its greatness was to extol himself. He measured himself with his Northern compeer, and decided without hesitation in his own favor."[32]

Tourgée exaggerated the crime of the Ku Klux Klan and the noble courage of freedmen like Nimbus. And yet he was certainly correct in realizing the futility of individual resistance, the kind of resistance that Nimbus attempts in *Bricks Without Straw*. Unable to shape a future for himself, to own land, to educate himself, to raise himself by his own bootstraps, to exercise the liberation legally granted him, or to combine with others in his own defense, Nimbus reverts to that last resort of all subservients—retaliation. He intends to proclaim his freedom, to denounce the Ku Klux Klan, to kill if necessary.

The irrational and cruel behavior of the Ku Klux Klan is vividly described when crippled Eliab Hill, Nimbus' closest friend, is brutally attacked. Tourgée records this scene in his usual melodramatic fashion, but the portrait of Eliab Hill as a kind of Black Christ dying for his race is nevertheless effective:

> His lips moved in prayer, the forgiving words mingling with the curses of his assailants: 'O God, my help and my shield! (*Here he is, God damn him!*) 'Forgive them, Father—' (I've got him!) 'They know not——a——h!'
>
> A long shrill shriek—the voice of a man overborne by mortal agony—sounded above the clamor of curses, and above the roar of the blazing church. There was a fall upon the cabin floor—the grating sound of a baby swiftly drawn along its surface—and one of the masked marauders rushed out dragging on the floor the preacher of the Gospel of Peace. The withered leg was straightened. The weakened sinews were torn asunder, and as his captor dragged him out into the light and flung the burden away, the limb dropped, lax and nerveless, to the ground. Then there were blows and kicks and curses from the crowd, which rushed upon him. In the midst, one held aloft a blazing brand. Groans and fragments of prayer came up through the din.[33]

Thus the strength of Nimbus, Eliab Hill, and those Negroes who supported them proves to be inadequate against the organized oppression of the Ku Klux Klan. Nimbus is forced to leave his home, realizing that if he wishes to exist at all, his departure from the South is the only course of action he can take. Having lived in an area in which the *state* has submerged his every aspiration and ambition, he knows that only the *nation* can help and protect him. But the *nation*—hesitant, uncertain of itself, ruled by shortsighted leaders—has refused to assume so great a responsibility. The leaders have helped to free the Negro, and now that he is free, they have demanded great things from him. They have demanded works of wisdom from an uneducated man; and, like the taskmaster in biblical times, they have told him that "*there shall no straw be given you, yet shall ye deliver the tale of bricks.*"[34]

Nimbus' exodus from his land of bondage attracts the sympathy of some of the more sensitive "royal gentlemen" in the South. Shifting the emphasis of his story, Tourgée now reports the effects that these brutalities have on the mind of a typical Southerner, Hesden Le Moyne. The character of Le Moyne is cut from the same pattern as Geoffrey Hunter's in *A Royal Gentleman*; his attitude, also, is reactionary and unaffected by the Civil War. He wishes no harm to the Negro, yet he anticipates no competition from him; the idea of social equality among races is to him incomprehensible. But because of his love for the schoolteacher Mollie Ainslie, and the atrocities committed against Nimbus and Eliab Hill, he begins to doubt his superiority. And when he supports certain Radical Republican principles, when he defends the colored people, when he is heedless of his mother's admonitions, he finds that he has "lost his rank, degraded his caste, and fallen from his high estate. From and after that moment he was held unworthy to wear the proud appellation, 'A Southern Gentleman.' "[35]

Le Moyne's conversion to the Northern point of view is akin to Lily Ravenel's (in J. W. De Forest's novel), for he too comes to recognize the need for national unity through the attitudes of his loved ones. And as in *Miss Ravenel's Conversion*, much of the tolerance and respect for the Negro is gained through education. When Lily Ravenel teaches Negro workers on a Southern plantation and watches the superior work they perform under the kind tutelage of her father, she grows convinced that the "superior manners" she so much respected in Louisiana gentleman are largely artifices. A similar disillusionment overcomes Le Moyne; but, unlike Lily Ravenel, he attempts to oppose Southern pride. He becomes Tourgée's martyr and thus his mouthpiece, decrying the doctrine of States' rights as the root of almost all the evil that the country has suffered.

To obviate the evils engendered by the poor Reconstruction policies of the national government, Tourgée proposes a plan: the government is to distribute a fund of money for education in proportion to the illiteracy of the different communities. The realization of this plan would, in addition to providing equal education for all people, help to create a more hospitable attitude on the part of the Southerners who would then not be solely responsible for the education of the colored man. Tourgée is now able to understand, if not agree with, the Southern white who claims that

. . . the Nation fostered and encouraged slavery; it gave it greater protection and threw greater safeguards around it than any other kind of property; it encouraged my ancestors and myself to invest the proceeds of generations of care and skill and growth in slaves. When the war ended it not only at one stroke dissipated all these accumulations, but it also gave to these men the ballot, and would now drive me, for my own protection, to provide for their education. This is unjust and oppressive. I will not do it, nor consent that it shall be done by my people or by my section alone.[36]

Tourgée realizes that his plan for national supervision of state schools will not necessarily prove the most effective.[37] Nor does he insist that it be the plan finally used. His chief desire is to stimulate an awareness of the need for nation-wide education; as the novel ends, Hesden Le Moyne is exhorting a Northern congressman to keep this idea uppermost in his mind. "Don't think of it as a politician in the little sense of that word," he says, "but in the great one. Don't try to compel the Nation to accept your view or mine, but spur the national thought by every possible means to consider the evil, to demand its cure, and to devise a remedy."[38]

Tourgée's primary object in writing *Bricks Without Straw* and *A Fool's Errand* was to present the issues of Reconstruction in the clearest possible light. To be outspoken in his denunciation of wrong; to persuade the indifferent Northerner of his responsibility to the Negro; to portray the nobility and potential greatness of the colored man who now, in the Reconstruction period, was a "racial outcast"—these were his intentions as an author. Both novels deserve a lasting place in any history of our literature; for, in addition to being dramatically compelling as narratives, they re-create Reconstruction in human terms more convincing than most other fiction of the period. They live as the records of a humane reporter whose insights into this complex period have been borne out by later historians and whose projected solution to the Negro's problems—federal aid to education in proportion to the degree of illiteracy in each state—is still being advanced by political leaders.

CHAPTER 6

The End of Political Autobiography

IN EACH of the novels we have considered, the figure of the "royal gentleman" has played an important role. Representing the proud Southerner as the resistant force to any progress in Reconstruction policies, Tourgée attempted to show both his salutary and pernicious effects on Southern culture. Above all, he presented him for the enlightenment of the Northern reader, who hardly comprehended such an intensity of pride. But this figure has always been observed from an alien point of view. Tourgée could never become a part of the life in North Carolina; he could never merely describe local folkways—though he was able to sympathize with and admire his Southern opponents— for he remained a judge in his writing as well as in life. In his next novel, *John Eax* (1882), Tourgée once again focuses on the post-bellum South. But rather than attempt another panoramic view, as he had in all his other Reconstruction novels, he turns his attention to Southern pride and makes it the substance of his tale; he struggles to shift his frame of reference, to place himself entirely within the context of the Southern aristocratic family.

I *John Eax and Mamelon*

John Eax is the story of a boy's rebellion against the established aristocracy of his family. The De Jeunettes, in the social hierarchy of the South, are people of the first rank. Like the Grandissimes in Cable's novel, they are a closely knit family; they inbreed; they protect one another from any antagonistic force; they consider themselves the gentry of the South; and they know that they are entirely self-sufficient. The young rebel, the narrator of the story, tells of an incident which vividly illustrates the strength that families like the De Jeunettes possessed: "Once when a Judge of more than ordinary nerve was riding through the circuit, and my ancestor for some drunken freak was committed to jail for contempt of court, there was a sudden mustering of forces, and before the Judge had left the bench, the jail was broken open and the prisoner set at liberty. It was done in broad, open day, and every one knew the culprits. They were the De Jeunettes."[1]

When Charles De Jeunette marries Alice Bain, the niece of his father's overseer, he does more than merely betray his family and incite it to anger. He causes the deaths of his disappointed parents and arouses the other members of his family to such a point of uncontrollable frenzy that they destroy his house and confiscate the livestock and property belonging to Alice Bain and her father. They become as violent as Ku Kluxers, Tourgée insists, because they realize that the worst opposition to their sanctity of caste is internal rebellion.

We are able to see the possibilities latent in such a conflict when we compare Tourgée's version with the more impressive treatment offered by George Washington Cable in "Belles Desmoiselles." Cable also uses the idea of ancestral pride in his poignant story. He creates a pompous, arrogant Southern aristocrat who wants to buy the home of his distant Indian cousin so that he may enlarge his own estate. But the cousin has too much family pride; he refuses to be ostracized by his relatives and does not sell his small house, even though he is offered $75,000. The adjacent Mississippi finally inundates part of the plantation, destroying the seven "belles desmoiselles," and the older "cavalier" dies of a broken heart.

Tourgée cannot resolve the conflict that exists between Charles De Jeunette and his family within the framework of his novel. He cannot, as Cable can in his work, retain his point of view and find some satisfactory answer—negative or positive—that grows out of the materials of his story. He resorts once again to a trite plot device; the young De Jeunette goes with Alice Bain to New York and discovers that she is the heiress to her great-grandfather's treasure. Her ancestor, John Eax, however, stipulates that she must retain the name Eax, and so Charles De Jeunette assumes the surname and travels with his wealthy wife to the Northwest. Alice Bain dies in childbirth, and De Jeunette, having fought heroically for the Union cause, returns and marries a typical Southern belle. Tourgée attempts to redeem his factitious ending by having the narrator claim that this was a new South he was returning to, that the old order was dying and a new one "was springing into life about [them]—the spirit of the North and the manhood of the South with its matchless elements."[2] But it is apparent that Tourgée, despite his avowed belief in social equality, was working in the literary tradition of Scott, a tradition which rested upon the class distinctions made in the English social system and which forbade a gentleman to marry the niece of his overseer. Having created a situation which called for a marriage between De Jeunette and Alice Bain, he was forced to recognize his higher commitment to the tradition which demanded wedlock between people of the same social caste; nevertheless, he also recognized that the preference for marrying someone of the same background is, after all, natural.

The novel published together with *John Eax* was *Mamelon, or The South Without the Shadow*. Like its companion volume, *Mamelon* is written from the Southerner's point of view. "The shadow was over all," Tourgée writes in the preface, "the shadow of Slavery and of its Children, Ignorance and War and Poverty. In the Shadow I wrote, contrasting it with the light." Paul Dewar, the Southern hero of the novel, serves in the war as a colonel; on his return home he discovers that he is financially ruined—not only is all his "slave property gone, but all debts builded on the faith of such property [are] generally valueless."[3]

Dewar works side by side with the Negroes in the tobacco fields, unable to adjust himself to postwar conditions in the South, until a Northerner, Dickinson, suggests that the two of them use the hickory and oak forest for the manufacturing of handles. Together they establish a handle factory, which is successful at first but finally fails in the depression of 1873. Completely ruined, Dewar attempts to shoot himself but is saved by the Northerner, who operates on the gunshot wound. Fortunately the bullet Dewar had intended for himself scars a rock in his archaeological collection, and after inspecting the stone, the men discover it to be corundum. Southerner and Northerner thus grow wealthy through mutual ingenuity and friendship, in a tale that is patently incredible.

Those parts of the novel that seem plausible are autobiographical. In February, 1871, Tourgée had formed the North Carolina Handle Company, but it failed in the panic of 1873 and "left him with liabilities of $30,000 and only a quantity of unsalable stock with which to meet them." It was not until June 20, 1876 that he was able to write a friend, "The monetary misfortunes of which you are already informed have given me two years of very hard work, though I can now see that they have been of great advantage to me."[4] When Tourgée stays close to fact, to personal experience—as in his description of Dewar's failure and depression over it—he is direct, forceful, and even moving. But when he attempts to write imaginatively—as in the preposterous conclusion of *Mamelon*—he is as unimpressive as most of the sentimental writers of his time.

II *Our Continent*

In the year that *John Eax* and *Mamelon* were published, Tourgée, his wife, and his daughter lived in Philadelphia. Tourgée, who had never been able to succeed financially in any of his various business ventures, was now originating a weekly magazine, *Our Continent*, "which proved more disastrous to him than that 'errand' of reconstruction days."[5] The journal merits some attention, for it is the clearest example of how closely Tourgée's literary, if not political, attitudes were shared by most late nineteenth-century authors. He had written his most effective novels, and *Our Continent* represents a turning point in his career: it clearly indicates the increasingly sentimental and commercial attitude Tourgée was to assume in his later fiction. "The Continent started," Tourgée wrote, "with the determination to present the readers in a weekly form the peculiar features and attractions of the best monthly magazine. Its conductor set before him as exemplars the great monthlies of our neighboring city because there were none elsewhere to compare with them in excellence. . . . The Continent was a pioneer. The attempt to embody the artistic and literary attractions of the modern monthly in weekly form had never before been made."[6]

The magazine was as large as the average monthly periodical—

a journal of sixteen pages—and contained the popular features characteristic of such productions: serial stories (by popular writers like Helen Campbell and E. P. Roe); short stories (by D. G. Brinton and Rebecca Harding Davis); poetry (by George Parsons Lathrop and George H. Boker); "Literary Notes"; "The Still Hour" (quotations); "The Household"; "In a Lighter Vein"; "The Bookshelf"; "Notes and Queries"; and special articles on timely subjects. The contributors were either local colorists or popular sentimentalists who were generally in sympathy with Tourgée's views about literature. Celia Thaxter, Frank B. Stockton, Harriet Beecher Stowe, H. H. Boyesen, Julian Hawthorne, Harriet Prescott Spofford, Joel Chandler Harris, Sarah Orne Jewett, and Mary Wilkins Freeman all wrote novels, stories, or poems for the magazine.

In addition, the periodical was a kind of barometer of public opinion, for Tourgée was quite openly catering to the taste of the public: "We shall go into the market for what we believe our readers most desire in art or literature and get it if we can. Our writers will be those who most delight our readers, our artists those whose works please most, if by any means their work is procurable."[7] Consequently, the chief interest that the public displayed toward literary figures becomes manifest in the published essays. "Was Emerson Cold?," "The Sister of Edgar A. Poe," "Night Shadows in Poe's Poetry," and "Henry James on American Traits" (by James Lane Allen) are the typical feature articles.

The tone of the magazine naturally reflected Tourgée's interests, and the ideas which we have discussed and seen illustrated in his novels are explicitly stated. His editorials are filled with commentaries on the South, countless defenses of the Negro, and passionate denunciations of the Republican party for failing to enact legislation leading to national education. But Tourgée did not write only of serious matters. He knew he was editing a popular magazine which had to sell in order to survive, and so he composed moral disquisitions on such different subjects as the excessive use of tobacco and alcohol, Mormonism, the value of home life, the duty of everyone to be a "citizen-king" and to take an active part in politics. In addition, he wrote poetry, but it was usually so overtly tendentious that it is hardly worth consideration:

"Enough! Enough! I waking cried:
"Oh, comrades! not in vain ye died!
"Let brambles hide each grave!
"Let mural tables fade.
"Ye need them not
"For Afric's child
"Knows not the name of slave."[8]

Tourgée labored arduously with the magazine. Often his working hours were so long he fell sick and was unable to continue writing.[9] He assured "the well-wishing prophets of evil" that the magazine was enjoying unusual success, but his statements were for the most part bravado.[10] Robert S. Davis, who had furnished the necessary funds at the inception of *Our Continent*, withdrew before the completion of the first volume and gave his interests to Tourgée for $10,000. In vain, Tourgée tried to receive financial aid from a friend, James Gordon Bennett; then in December, 1883, he moved to New York because of the opportunities there. He also changed his office for personal reasons; the major financial assistants in Philadelphia had been a liquor dealer and two Democrats.

By July, 1884, his sworn statement shows that the average monthly receipts from subscriptions were only $1,426; and the last issue was published on August 13, 1884. Later he was to write of the experiment: "A very rich man induced me in 1881 to engage with him in publishing the *Continent* magazine. When his extravagance and pretense had swamped what ought to have been a success, he dug out and I very foolishly undertook to resuscitate the corpse. Had I been brave enough to cut expenses down to bed-rock, I should have succeeded. But I wasn't. . . . It was a bad break—took everything and a lot more."[11]

III *The Last Report on Reconstruction*

Hot Plowshares, Tourgée's last Reconstruction novel, was serialized intermittently in *Our Continent* from July, 1882, until May, 1883; it was also published in book form by Fords, Howard, and Hulbert in the spring of 1883. Creatively, Tourgée attempted more in *Hot Plowshares* than he had in any other novel, for the book was "designed to give a review of the antislavery struggle by tracing its growth and the influences of the sentiment upon contrasted characters."[12] But, in spite of his audacious attempt, this new novel is prolix and sentimentally contrived and falls short of achieving Tourgée's aims. The prolixity and technical contrivances of the work can be in part explained by the fact that it was first written serially for *Our Continent*, in which the editor announced that "the story embraces a range of types almost entirely new and covers a period of American history hitherto so untouched by the novelist as to excite surprise as its richness in material is unfolded in 'Hot Plowshares.'"[13] The novel lacks continuity and firm structure, and too many of the chapters end with a "narrative hook" that promises more excitement in the next installment.

We are concerned in *Hot Plowshares* with story devices that frequently recur in nineteenth-century American fiction: the justification of the protagonist's genealogy and the theme of rightful inheritance. In the fiction of Reconstruction, these devices were used repeatedly. Vicious scalawags or carpetbaggers acted as overseers who attempted to disinherit the rightful owners of Southern estates, as in Thomas Nelson Page's *Red Rock*; or an ostensibly white man discovered that he possessed Negro blood and thereafter justified his new role as a colored man, as in Rebecca Harding Davis' *Waiting for the Verdict*.

Hilda Hargrove, the young heroine of Tourgée's novel, is led to believe that she is not actually the daughter of the liberal Southern gentleman Mervyn Hargrove, but rather the child of Hargrove's brother, a man who married a quadroon. She makes this discovery while attending a typical New England seminary. Sent there by Mervyn Hargrove, Hilda has won the love of her fellow students and has led a sheltered, happy, untroubled life. By using the seminary as the locale for part of his story, Tourgée is able to depict naturally the varying reactions of the students and teachers to the appalling news that Hilda possesses a taint of Negro blood. The revelation of Hilda's past becomes a test of character to which each figure in the book is subjected; it becomes a test of each individual's essential humanity and finally defines him as a human being. Her school friends reject her completely, and Tourgée expatiates at great length on the fact that these children have inherited their parent's prejudices.

He can, however, be optimistic; for there are men, Southerners as well as Northerners, who have been led into a state of uncertainty because of the abolitionist movement and the

Fugitive Slave Law. Martin Kortright, the hero of *Hot Plow-shares*, is one of these men; hearing of Hilda's exigency, he immediately hurries to her aid. Young Martin, the product of the American farm in Ohio, has seen his father liberalize his political position to become a staunch abolitionist. The intellectual conflict between Martin's father and Mervyn Hargrove that occupies the first half of Tourgée's novel is once again the typical conflict between the Northerner who has not experienced the problems of slavery at first hand and the sensitive, genuinely kind Southerner who is rooted in his tradition. Hargrove has considered the condition of the Negro for many years, and the most liberal opinion he can offer the older Kortright is: "If the government stands I don't see how slavery can help standing with it. . . . I wish we had never had slavery, nor the negro either; but having the negro, I don't see how we can get along without slavery."[14]

The irreconcilable attitudes of Hargrove and Kortright form the political background of the novel; the action, however, is forwarded by Hargrove's daughter Hilda. Now forced to suffer the same bigotry her father has been condoning, Hilda is unprepared for such an overwhelming challenge; she loses self-possession and escapes from the seminary. After presenting this contrived and melodramatic climax, Tourgée provides us with a rather protracted anticlimax; he quickly informs us that this kind of escape is only temporary. If apprehension and horror have been her first emotional responses to this new identity, Hilda soon accepts what she supposes to be her lot in life and returns to the seminary. Her stern resolution is unnecessary, however, for through the most adventitious and incredible circumstances she proves to be the daughter of Mervyn Hargrove: her aunt, a somnambulist and an insane woman, reveals to Martin Kortright's father particular love letters that Mervyn Hargrove had written to his wife, letters that reveal Hilda as their daughter. Thus Hilda is of Caucasian blood, is now able to marry Martin Kortright, and she remains to the end a victim, a passive rather than an active heroine.

At this point we need not dwell on the "artistic" limitations of *Hot Plowshares*: the verbosity, fortuitous incidents, awkward use of the supernatural and incredible idealization of the teen-age heroine are some of the more prominent elements that mar this excessively long novel. Of more significance, for our purposes, is the fact that the novel does not even succeed in promoting Tourgée's political views. *Hot Plowshares* leaves a total effect on our mind that is negative, for we feel that the most satisfactory solution for an individual is not to be a Negro at all. When Hilda Hargrove discovers that she is really white, all the sympathetic characters (and this should include the reader) sigh with relief; she now has none of the problems which confront the Negro. Having created all kinds of dramatic possibilities by presenting a pure white girl with the sudden discovery that purity lies only in the color of one's skin, Tourgée evades his literary commitment by destroying the very situation he has fashioned.

In the preface to *Hot Plowshares*, Tourgée outlined the scope and purpose of his Reconstruction novels:

> Many years ago the author conceived the idea that he might aid some of his fellow-countrymen and country-women to a juster comprehension of these things [the conflict between North and South, between the Southern aristocrat and the newly-freed Negro] by a series of works which should give, in the form of fictitious narrative, the effects of the distinct and contrasted specific periods of the great transition. Beginning their preparation in 1867, in the midst of the fading glare of revolution, on the very spot where one of the great armies of the rebellion surrendered, he has worked patiently and honestly and zealously to complete his analyses of the representative groups of character. By birth and education he became intuitively familiar with the Northern life. Born upon the Western Reserve, the irresponsible years of boyhood and youth were almost equally divided between the East and the West. They were years of fruitful thought and unconscious observation. From the close of the war until 1880 he resided continuously at the South, and studied with the utmost care, and from a standpoint of peculiar advantage, the types of the expiring and coming eras.
> . . . The period covered by the . . . series of six volumes extends from twenty years before the war until twenty years after it. . . . In chronological order they would stand as follows: "Hot Plowshares," "Figs and Thistles," "A Royal Gentleman," "A Fool's Errand," "Bricks Without Straw," "John Eax."[15]

This statement of aims was not so clearly formulated when Tourgée began to write *A Royal Gentleman*; in 1867 he had no idea that he would write a "series" of novels dealing with Reconstruction, nor did he have any special "chronological order" in mind. Moreover, there is no particular profit in reading the series in the chronological sequence to which Tourgée refers, for those novels—*Hot Plowshares* and *Figs and Thistles*—which do not deal directly with Reconstruction are artificially historical; in no way do they serve even as background for Tourgée's more important fiction. They are as poorly contrived and as sentimentally stated as most historical fiction, and they have no significant comment to make that permits us to overlook their excessive sentimentality.

The works which present Tourgée's individual interpretation of post-bellum problems are *A Fool's Errand* and *Bricks Without Straw;* they are his immediate response to conditions he witnessed in the South and thus have an historical validity that is grounded on personal experience. In terms of fiction, Tourgée is most effective when he reports the Reconstruction South he knew so well. His "direct style is forceful, trenchant, interesting," as his publisher, J. B. Ford, wrote him, "but his 'high toned' or philosophical style is apt to get labored and somewhat involved."[16] In *A Royal Gentleman, Figs and Thistles,* and *Hot Plowshares,* Tourgée insists on discussing the "moral" and social implications of his story—he insists on using his labored "philosophical" style. As a consequence, situations which begin dramatically in those novels end with Tourgée's unnecessary commentary on them. Certainly *A Fool's Errand* and *Bricks Without Straw* are not entirely free of this fault either—they too are marred by technical crudities; but in these two novels Tourgée's verbose disquisitions are counterbalanced by the convincing—the largely reportorial—story he has to tell.

When Tourgée began to write *A Royal Gentleman* in 1867 he was not only trying to "aid some of his fellow countrymen . . . to a juster comprehension" of the Negro's problems in the South. He was beginning a personal investigation of the reasons for the failure of Radical Republicanism in the South; his writings are as much an accounting to himself as they are a "public service." As a record of his own political failure, his Reconstruction novels form a political autobiography that was not attempted by any of his contemporaries.

One contemporary, of course, did advocate equal rights for Negroes as forcefully as Tourgée. In the 1880's George Washington Cable vigorously championed the civil rights of the freedman. "Convinced as he was by the early 1870's that slavery had been a great moral wrong and sharply aware that the effects of slavery reached down to his own time, [Cable] took the attitude of one sincerely contrite for the errors of the society to which he belonged and was eager to make whatever amends might be possible."[17]

Cable, in essays like "The Freedman's Case in Equity" (1884) and "The Silent South" (1885), was more eloquent than Tourgée and thus more convincing; but perhaps the chief reason why important literary figures of the South responded to him more than they did to Tourgée was that he was a Southerner and had rejected many of his "inherited attitudes and established institutions." He was not a carpetbagger who seemed to Southerners to be only a political opportunist manipulating Negroes for his own political ends, and even though he was considered an outsider by many Southerners, he said that he felt a "particular obligation to speak and write on the Southern problem . . . because he was a Southerner and by descent and his own participation was involved with the institutions and attitudes belonging to the South." Like Tourgée he "searched for the ethical and moral answers" to slavery, but he did not debate "technicalities and constitutionality."[18] Cable, together with Walter Hines Page (editor of the *State Chronicle* [1889] and author of the novel *The Southerner* [1909]), "started Southern self-criticism, and since then the South has had a growing school of nonscalawag liberals, all working in line with the national democratic ideals. They have been violently denounced. . . . Even today they are denounced by perhaps the majority of Southerners."[19]

The attitude of superiority to the Negro that Tourgée and Cable attacked certainly still exists—in the North as well as the South. We need only glance at the daily newspaper to be aware of the fact that many politicians and people still refuse to grant the Negro equality. And though Tourgée was perhaps excessively pessimistic when he wrote in 1902 that "unless God intervenes there is no other fate before the colored American" but subordination,[20] enough men devoted to the myth of white supremacy have reminded us that some of the same barriers to bringing about equality in this country still exist.

IV *National Aid to Education*

Tourgée realized after his experiences in North Carolina that the complete rehabilitation of the South would be a long, arduous process. He realized, now that the war was an unpleasant memory of the recent past, that the Northerner desired only to forget its causes and results as soon as possible.[21] To Tourgée the Northern citizen could not evade his responsibility, for the white minorities of the South "had nullified the law and defied the national power" ever since the end of the Civil War, and they could not be trusted to determine the future of the Negro. In the decades to come, the Northerners would have to be the guarantors of the colored man's peace and prosperity, asking themselves *not* "What shall we do with the Negro?" but rather "What will the Negro permit us to do with him?"[22]

Consequently, Tourgée continued throughout the 1880's his extreme support of the Negro. In 1884 he published *An Appeal to Caesar*,[23] a carefully documented tract which was written with the hope that the Republicans, if elected, would put into effect its proposals on national education. In *An Appeal to Caesar*, Tourgée set down his final and complete statement in regard to education.

Tourgée recognized that many legislators desired national aid to education, but they were too willing "to waive all questions of form, method, and detail in order to secure a general concurrence in a liberal appropriation of public funds for the purpose of promoting primary education in the various States, and thereby reducing promptly and effectually the present ratio of illiteracy."[24] Tourgée, who therefore directed his attention to the method of application, said that the states were not to control the funds allocated to education; money was "to be distributed, on the basis of illiteracy, *to the various townships and school districts in which free primary schools shall have been in active operation for a specified period* during the time covered by the appropriation, *and having a specified average attendance.*"[25] Tourgée felt that "very little of the ornate machinery which is found in the Northern public school is needed. . . . In the administration of this fund the utmost economy is absolutely essential."[26] Also, he insisted that his proposal "must provide with absolute certainty that the fund shall be expended for the promotion of primary education and for no other purpose."[27] Tourgée urged primary education for both whites and Negroes, though the schools did not have to be integrated. He clearly points out that "in case the State within which any district is located prescribes separate schools for white and colored pupils, then the [equal] number of colored illiterates would entitle it to receive in like manner the support of a school for colored children; and neither of these sums shall, under any circumstances, be used to aid a school for the benefit of the other race."[28] In the expenditure of the fund, the national government ought "to avoid trespassing in the least degree upon the specific domain of the State," but on the other hand, the government must never "place the fund under the control of any State officials or State legislature."[29]

It is noticeable that education is the only solution Tourgée offers for the improved status of the Negro and that his educational program is far more moderate than the immediate demands he championed at the 1868 Constitutional Convention. His political failure in the South had taught him to be more cautious in urging certain measures, and he now fully understood the difficulties implicit in the educational program he proposed. In *A Fool's Errand,* in *Bricks Without Straw,* and in the tract *An Appeal to Caesar,* he presented a picture of the Southern condition that clearly indicates why his ultimate decision was for gradualism. The South was a self-contained kingdom, he observed; it was a land whose cherished traditions no foreign idea could penetrate. White settlers did not tend to move North, the Negroes themselves suffered from an even greater inertia, and foreigners from either the Northern states or Europe hardly ever emigrated South. With bitterness he recorded, in *An Appeal to Caesar,* that in all the Southerners' "frantic appeals of the last twenty years for immigration there will be noted by a careful reader an undertone defining what the desired immigrant must *not* be. He must not come bringing with him new ideas. He must not come with any thought that is not in harmony with the civilization that surrounds him. He must come prepared to divest his mental and moral nature of all the impressions that they have received hitherto, and to receive and adopt the feelings and sentiments of the vicinage in which he expects to dwell."[30]

His program for national aid to education was never considered by legislators, for Cleveland became President and "deemed it unnecessary to take any special action with respect to Negroes."[31] In both his first and second terms "Cleveland undoubtedly believed with most Americans, North and South, that the Southern question should be handled by Southerners."[32]

V *Political Journalism*

The sixty thousand dollars Tourgée received from the publication of his books was gone by 1884, largely spent in the publication of *Our Continent*; his estate in Mayville, New York, which he bought in 1881, and the future sales of his novels were mortgaged; and many debts still remained. In an attempt to earn additional money, as well as to advertise his political ideas, he began on December 13, 1884, an association with the Chicago *Inter Ocean* (March 25, 1872–May 10, 1914) that lasted until September, 1898.

Tourgée's writings for this Republican newspaper were of a political nature, and they prove to be as uninteresting as most topical journalism is to later generations of readers. When Cleveland was elected President in 1884, Tourgée, who realized that his proposals for national education would not be put into practice, addressed a series of articles to the Democrat President. Political denunciations of an intensely personal character, they reveal Tourgée in his most unattractive role—that of an unrelenting, intolerant partisan. "You are neither a scholar, a statesman, nor a soldier," he wrote about Cleveland on December 13, 1884, "and are entitled to no little credit for setting up no claim to any such distinction."[33] Throughout the weekly essays he tirelessly attacked Cleveland:

Queerly enough, however, you began to refer to yourself as an honest man. . . . Your regard for the rest of mankind is based solely on their relations to yourself—your comfort, success, and convenience. . . . It is not your fault that you have never known the sentiment of friendship. . . . The Republicans no longer fear you; the Populists despise you; the South curses you; the West threatens you; the East pities you; the mugwump has ceased to chant your praises; the free traders even denounce you. There is no sort of question but the Democracy would raise $500,000 in a week if you would take it, resign, get out of the White House, and let the compact and resolute Illinoisan [Thomas

> Brackett Reed], who presides over the Senate take the steering
> oar for the rest of the trip. . . . You march to fate over the
> ruins of the party you have wrecked by sheer incapacity.[34]

The author of these vindictive, puerile, and unimaginative
essays was constantly defended by the editor of the *Inter Ocean*.
"The articles," he remarked, "are written by one who has made
a closer study of Mr. Cleveland and his character than any
other man living, and by one who has been in the very front
of every fierce political battle of the last thirty years."[35] Tourgée
continued his attacks on Cleveland and the Democrats in another series of essays, now entitled "A Child of Luck." "So many
calls have been made for Siva [Tourgée's pseudonym]," the
editor noted, "that the old veteran politician has been induced
to take up his pen again."[36] And so Tourgée began his political
vilification once more, claiming that he was a "moral and political
philosopher, weighing and determining the effect of facts rather
than compiling the immaterial facts themselves. He is doing
for 'The Man of Destiny,' precisely what Cicero did for
Marcus Antoninus, with similar purpose."[37] Now that Cleveland
had not fulfilled the destiny that the Presidency affords every
incumbent, Tourgée could only regard him as "A Child of Luck,
begotten of chance and born of froward Accident."[38]

But Tourgée did not write only attacks on Cleveland for the
Inter Ocean. On September 26, 1885, he began another group
of essays, called "Letters to a Mugwump," and signed them
Trueman Joyce. Addressed to "One of the Undistinguished Too
Pure for Politics," a certain C. Marcellus Montague, they urged
him to associate himself with some political party since no
man should divorce himself from an interest in politics. Later,
in May, 1888, Tourgée wrote weekly articles for the *Inter Ocean*
and entitled them "A Bystander's Notes." In these essays of a
general nature, innumerable and varied subjects are covered:
the defense of the carpetbagger, education, politics and religion,
civil service, "waving the bloody shirt," the South, book reviews,
foreign affairs, an extended commentary on James Fenimore
Cooper and American literature, frequent denunciations of
the Democratic party and defenses of the Republican, and,
most commonly, analyses of Negro problems. So fervent was
his sympathy for the colored man that in October, 1891, he
appealed to the public for the formulation of a "Citizen's Equal

Rights Association." This was an attempt to act rather than merely to speak in behalf of the Negro; but, as with his business schemes, this idea also culminated in failure.

The series, "A Bystander's Notes," ended in September, 1898; and, with its conclusion, Tourgée ceased to write for the *Inter Ocean*. His journalistic ventures were indeed ephemeral by any standard, revealing the least attractive aspects of his character—his insolence and independence. One conclusion is certain: if Tourgée had been actively hostile to the South during his residence in North Carolina, he became even more antagonistic in the 1880's and 1890's. His splenetic articles read like the vehement and ill-tempered gestures of a bilious man who has lost whatever audience he once had and now appeals only to the most partisan reader. Personal failure in his political and literary life aggravated rather than attenuated his hostility to Northern indifference toward the Negro, and his blind support of the Republican party was so obstinate that he was incapable of viewing the political scene with anything resembling objectivity.[39] Cleveland's unusually fine record itself serves as a sufficient rebuttal to most of his critic's animadversions.

CHAPTER 7

In a Minor Key

TOURGÉE, having written *A Fool's Errand* and *Bricks Without Straw*, had recorded what he had seen in the South in bold, stark terms; and now, though he had committed himself to the life of a novelist, he found himself with little to say that was original. When the last chapter of *Hot Plowshares* appeared in *Our Continent* in May, 1883, Tourgée had finished his series of Reconstruction novels. He did not seriously use the South for fictive purposes again; he now turned to the North and created imaginative tales which are hardly distinguishable from the mass of inferior fiction that appeared in the popular magazines of the 1880's and 1890's. Without politics as the central concern of his fiction, he was merely another third-rate writer catering to the public taste. The realistic elements that had redeemed his Reconstruction novels from their excessive sentimentality were absent from his later work, for which he relied solely on his imagination. Without political issues, his novels became sentimental fabrications, and though he believed in 1883 that "the life [the novelist] portrays he must have seen and felt in order to be realistically represented," his own active life was only a reminiscence now. He turned inward to his imagination and found it surprisingly barren.

I *Literary Theory*

Before discussing Tourgée's later fiction we ought to consider the literary milieu in which he was writing during the 1880's and 1890's. From this point on his fiction is indistinguishable from that of the commercially successful writers of his time; and his sympathy with their minor efforts, along with his outspoken hostility toward the highly imaginative work of major American authors, indicates the direction his own fiction took during this period of bad popular taste.

With the exception of Mark Twain, the major novelists of Tourgée's time were not of the South, nor were they interested in writing of that area. Much to Tourgée's chagrin, two of his most imaginative and gifted contemporaries were in New York and England, writing tales of urban life. Tourgée's vindictive comments regarding James, Howells, and other realists were so frequent that it becomes apparent to us that his objections were not solely literary. Rarely does he consider the artistic quality of their works; it is with the matter, the idea, that he is concerned. He had little patience or sympathy with the scrupulous attention being paid to the subtleties of character, to the nuances of human motivations. "What is termed the analysis of character in these works," he wrote in his magazine, *Our Continent* (1882-84), "is usually only a skillful use of paradoxes. The more absurdly inconsistent the motives and conduct attributed to a character the more subtle is the skill attributed to the author."[1] This statement is, of course, a standard defense of his own melodramatic writings. Tourgée, like other sentimentalists, does not create characters—he describes types. He concentrates exclusively on the action of his story and avoids the complexities of character development. "It is the poet of action whose clutch on the human soul is eternal, not the professor of analytics or the hierophant of doubt and uncertainty."[2]

An author like James, consequently, suffers greatly under the barb of Tourgée's criticism, for he deals with "morbid anatomy." Though his delineation of the rich "may be very real life . . . it is the life of a vacuum"; finally, "whatever his art may represent, it has no fellowship with the noblest and deepest facts of life." James, in Tourgée's opinion, was concerned with insignificant international problems hardly worth the attention of the American novelist: "Mr. James has looked at us through the large end of his opera glass, till convinced we are small enough for the microscopical examination he has inaugurated. . . . Till some gleam of spirituality is added he must remain artist, but never can become creator."[3]

Most local colorists were not sympathetic to James.[4] In his critical work *Hawthorne*, James had attacked ante-bellum American literature as being unduly provincial; and the special character of local color was precisely its provinciality. Furthermore, James disapproved of historical fiction in general, and Southern writers prided themselves on their faithful reminiscences of ante-bellum conditions. When Sarah Orne Jewett sent her historical novel *The Tory Lover* to James, he was remarkably direct in his denunciation of the genre:

> The "historic" novel is, for me, condemned even in cases of labour as delicate as yours, to a fatal *cheapness*, for the simple reason that the difficulty of the job is inordinate and that a mere *escamotage*, in the interest of ease, and of the abysmal public naivete become inevitable. You may multiply the little facts that can be got from pictures and documents, relics and prints as much as you like—*the* real thing is almost impossible to do and in its essence the whole effect is as nought: I mean the invention, the representation of the old *consciousness*, the soul, the sense, the horizon, the vision of individuals in whose minds half the things that make ours, that make the modern world were non-existent. You have to think with your modern apparatus a man, woman—or rather fifty—whose own thinking was intensely otherwise conditioned, you have to simplify back by an amazing tour de force—and even then it's all humbug. But there is a shade of the (even then) humbug that *may* amuse. The childish tricks that take the place of any such conception of the real job in the flood of Tales of the Past that seems of late to have been rolling over our devoted country—these ineptitudes have, on a few recent glances, struck me as creditable to no one concerned.[5]

Joel Chandler Harris thought James was "the most delightful literary snob of the period,"[6] an opinion with which other Southerners agreed. Harris, as a typical Southern writer of the 1880's, was hardly affected by the new literary experiments of James and Howells; he could not think of the South in realistic terms, and the influences which affected his craft were old-fashioned. Like Thomas Nelson Page, he was attracted to the eighteenth- and nineteenth-century English writers—Addison, Steele, Goldsmith, Thackeray, and Dickens—and to the older authors of the South before the war. He rejected, for the most part, such New England writers as Emerson, preferring Scott and Cooper.[7]

However different Tourgée's conception of the South was from that of post-bellum authors, his literary technique was identical. The authors who were to affect his own craft were the same authors who influenced writers of Reconstruction. Among Americans, Tourgée's greatest debt was to Cooper. In an extended tribute to the American "Wizard," he noted that he would

> . . . never cease to be grateful for the fact that he heard Cooper's novels read and commented upon, in his early boyhood, by [his] grandmother. . . . No doubt her comments and the narrative with which she supplemented the tales the boy read enabled him to appreciate more clearly than many others the realism of Cooper's descriptions both of life and conditions. . . . If we desire to have a people worthy of Anglo-Saxon ideals in their home, private morals, and public virtue, in the American Republic of the future, we can be sure of one thing—that the conceptions of love, truth, and purity found in Cooper's fiction will not smutch it.[8]

Tourgée thought of Cooper as the great American writer, and he was proud to carry on the tradition of the historical novelist. Like Cooper, he placed all of his novels in some historical context, attempting to advance a social idea. He too was fond of narrative and all the plot devices that help to move the narrative along: flight and pursuit (in *A Fool's Errand*), disguises (in *A Royal Gentleman* and *Hot Plowshares*), and secret escapes (in *Bricks Without Straw, Hot Plowshares,* and *John Eax*). Like Cooper, he had little regard for form and technique. His emphasis was primarily on content.

Many of Cooper's literary faults are Tourgée's: his use of stereotypes rather than genuine characters, his lack of humor, his unreal dialogue. True love is inevitably rewarded in Tourgée's sentimental novels. Whenever he criticized the realists or naturalists—the "morbid anatomists" as he characterized them— it was their description of women to which he most violently objected. Hardy, for example, expressed his "cool sensualism" in "decorous ingenuousness, combined with ignorance of what woman really is, in soul, feeling and purpose."[9] Invariably Tourgée would refer to Cooper as the novelist who championed morality in the novel. "As for the realistic adultery which modern fiction would substitute for romantic love," he remarked, it may lack Cooper's "silliness," but it lacks too his "sweetness." The life "which is fed upon it may be self-reliant and cynical—it may know the world and comprehend its shame—but all the same it will be rotten."[10]

Tourgée did not disapprove of James's subject matter, but objected to his supposed lack of acquaintance with American material; from his point of view, James was actually not "realistic" enough. Tourgée's real antipathy was reserved for those writers like Zola who chose for their literary canvas the slums and its inhabitants. He had no patience with novelists who did not uplift the spirit of man, who did not envisage a brighter future despite the present chaos. In the final scenes of Howells' *A Modern Instance* and of Zola's *Nana,* Tourgée saw only despair. The subject matter of *Nana* was not fit for the novel form, and its conclusion was inexcusable. Howells had turned "anatomist" (in *A Modern Instance*) and had chosen "hopelessly common and uninteresting subjects, more for the sake of demonstrating his own power of delineating to the minutest nerve-fibre, every shade of vulgarity and meanness and narrowness, than for any personal enjoyment in the work."[11] Truth in fiction, Tourgée felt, was "simply a possible life framed in a true environment. This life may be good or bad, high or low, worthy or mean, as the author may prefer, but it must be consistent with its environment and consistent with the known facts of the age in which it is represented as having existed."[12]

Tourgée's insistence on fidelity to environment is a significant indication of how much he was responding to the literary mood of the 1880's. Local color is worthless if it does not seem to report environmental conditions accurately; Tourgée knew this, and he was proud of his intimate knowledge of the South and particularly of Southern character. He objected to James's comments in *Hawthorne* about the absence in American life of the right sort of matter for romance writing. James had said, in Tourgée's paraphrased and partially distorted language, that "there are in this new country no castles, no storied ruins, no memories of eld, and particularly—oh, fatal defect!—no hereditary caste, no social class guarded by such impenetrable barriers that even love cannot find out the way, and hence the opportunities for touching or tragic positions are hard to find in our cis-Atlantic life."

Tourgée found James's observations too limited. "How little such critics know of the real element of interest in imaginative composition!" he said, once again offering the sentimentalist's confession. "It is one, one only, and that is *the human heart*, its pains and passions, its strengths and weaknesses, its longings and more than all its love. All else is but a foil and garb to this. Storied urn or stately tower affects us not at all, their descriptions are obtrusive and we skip them when once our interest is warmed in the hero and the heroine." Yet, despite his insistence on the "love" of "the human heart"—a love which has little to do with understanding—Tourgée refused to admit that American life suffered from a dearth of "romantic" materials. Instead, he claimed that it

> offers richer field for romantic incident than does English or most European society. The social relations of the sexes are more free with us, and the play of feeling is less restricted; our society is seething with change, while that of the old world is cast into rigid moulds, drilled into lines from which it is rare for one to step forth. Violent fluctuations are there uncommon, and their effects on character difficult to see. The contrary is notoriously true with us. Hence our country presents a vast diversity of personality and an uncomparable field for observation to the acute observer.
>
> Add to this that so many of our types are new, the outgrowth of a generation of the blood of all nations, under wholly novel conditions, presenting infinite facets of positive character, and all shades and sorts of positions and ambitions. Here is matter, excellent matter, more than abundant, for the writer who would hold the mirror up to nature and show this generation in its form and pressure.
>
> As to scenery, who can pretend but that if we want it, it is simply unsurpassed in variety and strength? Memories of the past, too, are not wanting, of a past as dear to us, and to millions of the human race whom we do not count among us, as any the old world can offer. With all these at hand, what need to fear that the richer veins of romance are not among the hidden treasures of the continent.[13]

It is a commonplace in literary history to be wary of the criticism of a practicing novelist or poet; usually the author's criticism reveals more of himself than of the work criticized. This is certainly true of Tourgée, for it is a little unfair to condemn an author like James for having "no fellowship with the noblest and deepest facts of life"[14] simply because he is not an historical novelist or a "novelist with a purpose." In addition, when an author begins speaking of the pains and passions, the strengths and weaknesses, and the longings and loves of the human heart, he is being too vague to be of much service. His reiterated praise of the newness of many of the American types (like the Negro) and of the novel conditions of living in this country is an obvious defense of Tourgée's own writings. Without the freed Negro, the recalcitrant Southern white, the carpetbagger, and the whole texture of the Reconstruction period, Tourgée's interest for us would be lost.

Tourgée was, after all, a polemicist and journalist who had to remain close to historical fact in order to produce readable works of fiction. His imagination was not particularly fertile, and his evaluation of artistic productions was often based on their fidelity to external experiences. When asked whether his novels were fair reflections of Southern life, he thought the question a challenge to his integrity as a human being and writer. "The novelist who does not seek honestly and faithfully to make his work true in every sense is a libeler who is all the more contemptible because he stands beyond the pale of the law." The novelist's obligation is akin to the historian's, for the duty "which rests upon the novelist in the depiction of sentiment and motive is precisely the same as rests upon the historian in the narration of mere facts. He is bound *voir dire,* more solemn than by any oath, to depict the life he professes to give as he believes it to be, and to attempt to delineate no life of which he has not had an intimate knowledge."[15]

In his magazine, *Our Continent,* and throughout his writings, Tourgée condemned the important writers of his time for their inordinate concern with the more unpleasant emotions and actions in life; but his own memorable writing is just that which involves terrorism and hatred and their pernicious effects on mankind. He could not rely solely on his imagination, nor be satisfied only with the aesthetic values of a literary work; for to Tourgée the novel that was pure art, that had no message, that did not speak directly to the reader of some significant issue was inferior. "A novel without a purpose is the counterpart of a man without an object," he wrote in 1883. "One written for mere amusement may be either good or bad, but at the very best, is only the lowest form of art."[16] The work of Zola and Howells, in his opinion, was essentially false, narrow, crude; it robbed life of its noblest aspirations and paralyzed "its progress toward heroic achievement, by substituting for self-sacrificing endeavor mere petulant, self-pitying submission, not to a sublime and overwhelming fate but to an innumerable host of petty ills." Tourgée believed that there was nothing worthy of the novelist's pen in the trivial annoyances of life, unless it was "to bring into clearer relief some noble quality which lifts man or woman above such petty ills."[17]

II *Minor Fiction*

The aesthetic premise on which Tourgée based the writing of his later novels was clear and, as usual, negatively phrased: "The theory that the novelist should simply reproduce the life he meets with, dirt and all, the only test of merit being the accuracy of the delineation and the brightness of the dialogue, is the most degrading view of the domain of art that has ever been formulated."[18] All of the novels that we are about to consider were written with a definite principle in mind, one which maintained that "the only true romance is that which is built upon those rare occurrences which are the result of a series of coincidences, and that pure realism is always to be avoided, save in historical matters."[19]

Rare occurrences and coincidences do indeed prevail in these works, and the reader's willingness to suspend his disbelief is strained inordinately. In *Black Ice* (1887) the tales of King Arthur's knights are brought up to date when, in a melodramatic climax, the hero rescues a somnambulist who has wandered to her baby's grave on an ice-capped mountain. Tourgée begins this tale effectively by remaining close to actual experience. The village that is described is obviously Mayville, New York, where Tourgée himself had bought a home, "Thorheim," in 1881 and where he was to live from 1884 until 1897; the lake, covered by black ice, is Chatauqua; the stern though kindly Dr. Colton is based on Dr. William Chace, to whom the book is dedicated; and the Reynolds family is clearly the author's. Tourgée draws the quiet picture of upstate New York in a rather attractive, subdued manner. But he soon resorts to artificial and factitious narrative as he describes a faultless heroine, Helen Somers, tending wounded soldiers during the Civil War; various children engaged in daring escapades on the black ice; and a hero, Percival Reynolds, who saves the life of Helen Somers by climbing mountains to discover her mourning at the grave of her child. Tourgée, at an early point in the novel, criticizes the realists by saying that "they tell us that fiction is of necessity limited by its sterile commonplaces to laborious self-dissection and elaborated display of the results of morbid mental anatomy."[20] He proceeds to illustrate his scorn of the emphasis that James and Howells were placing on character by writing *Black Ice*; but all he does offer is, as one critic has suggested, "a hodge-podge of mystery, suspense, fortuitous combinations of events, horror, and crime."[21]

Equally preposterous is *Button's Inn*, the Gothic novel Tourgée wrote in the same year. In it, the leading figure, Jack Button, murders in self-defense but returns years later to expiate his crime by aiding the victim's son; through a conversion to Mormonism, Button has discovered "that peace which passes all understanding." As in *Black Ice*, the locale of the story is Tourgée's new surroundings in upstate New York—Button's Inn had once been an actual inn northwest of Mayville—and once again the part of the novel describing the quiet life of this area is effective. But the book concentrates on the religious conversion of Jack Button to Mormonism, for Tourgée is trying to persuade the reader of the importance of love and trust in human relationships.

The ethical tone that pervades the book is not new in Tourgée's fiction—humanitarianism is a characteristic of all his heroes—but now it becomes obtrusively dominant and tendentious, the most notable feature of all his later works. Together with this emphasis on the proper moral conduct in human affairs, Tourgée stresses the significance of individualism by endowing his secondary hero, the young Ozro Evans, with inventive genius. Evans, who is the child of the woman for whose love Jack Button committed murder, invents a new kind of pin which is eventually so successful that Evans grows wealthy. Tourgée himself had, throughout his life, an irresistible inclination towards invention and had tried his hand at an all-steel harness for horses, iron posts, new brands of wrenches, a hydraulic motor, and other similar devices, none of which proved financially successful.

In *Button's Inn*, Tourgée asks for renewed faith in religion and individualism, condemning the absence of self-reliance in American life. "The presence of the multitude crushes out individuality," he asserts. "It may quicken the pulse, sharpen the wit, and improve the externals, but it breaks down the confidence of man in his own conclusions, motives, aspirations, and beliefs."[22] Tourgée's plea for humanitarianism and individualism is excessive; his fictional description of Jack Button, who wishes "to do good to those whom he had injured—to repair the evil he had wrought,"[23] and of Ozro Evans, a creative individual, is banal and melodramatic. Furthermore, he compounds the implausibility of his tale by burdening the story with other improbable elements: a ghost who is really a living person, a seduction, inherited money, a villain (Jack Button) who repents his evil ways, and a happy ending in which Ozro Evans wins the fair young lady of the novel.

The proper assortment of crime, the supernatural, piety, and romance explains why *Black Ice* and *Button's Inn*—both appearing in 1887—had a certain popularity with the general public. But from 1888 until his death, the sales of Tourgée's novels were extremely limited. Fiction, in the 1880's, had become "almost a matter of human geography, for the new writers seemed intent upon doing little more than describe in simple language the many diversities of the national scene"; Tourgée was still writing melodramatic novels "whose dreamy softness [had] satisfied the taste of mid-century America" but which were now obsolete."[24]

When Tourgée returned to the South as a setting for his fiction he was more successful, although his later novels never recaptured the intense historical immediacy of *A Fool's Errand* and *Bricks Without Straw*. In 1888 he wrote *Eighty-Nine; or The Grandmaster's Story*, which is in part a veiled denunciation of the Standard Oil Company; one of the characters in the novel has lost his possessions because of his active opposition to the "Rock Oil Company," to whose monopolistic practices he openly objects. The central subject of the book, however, is the evil of white supremacy as represented by the Ku Klux Klan. Royal Owen, Tourgée's hero, is a Georgian, a typical Southern gentleman, who promises his father that he will attempt to aid the South in the future and thus originates the "Order of the Southern Cross." Tourgée models this organization on the Ku Klux Klan, but he has Owen and other sympathizers urging "peaceful revolution" instead of the active aggression of the Klan. Members are allowed no weapons but may curb the undue political advancement of the Negro through the law. Tourgée is arguing for social and economic justice in *Eighty-Nine*: the "Order of the Southern Cross" is his solution to the abuse of Southern supremacy, and legal justice is his method for combating monopolies like the "Rock Oil Company."

Eighty-Nine indicates Tourgée's relentless interest in the political problems of his time. Though he wrote in this same period melodramatic novels like *Black Ice* and *Button's Inn* —both of which were obvious commercial ventures—his chief interest remained in the field of politics. *Eighty-Nine* repeats some of his standard attitudes toward Southern "egotism" and supremacy, his views on national education, his denunciations of Grover Cleveland.

In another volume, *Letters to a King*, which was also published in 1888, Tourgée continues to emphasize the need for legal justice and for political awareness on the part of every citizen. Comprised of chauvinistic essays which had appeared in religious journals, the book illustrates Tourgée's basic assumption that "politics is the broadest, richest and most important field of Christian endeavor."[25] Tourgée deplores the absence of ethical principles in politics, noting that Americans "have so thoroughly divorced religion from politics that" they "do not regard ethical principles as applying to political action."[26] Throughout the volume Tourgée explores various types of political corruption— office seeking, the buying of votes, political bossism—and chastises the individual citizen for the waning of political morality: "It is not alone the republican theory of government that is on trial in our country, but the American people—the Sovereign power of the land—as well."[27] These statements, so tedious in their political obviousness and nationalistic sincerity, recur throughout the book.

The moralistic tone so evident in Tourgée's minor works was repeated ceaselessly and with no self-consciousness. Every aspect of his personal life could be used as an excuse for moral disquisition; every aspect could be converted into an adventure. To the lawyer, for example,

> the days of romance are by no means a thing of the past. The daily facts of his life are more wonderful than the legends of King Arthur's time . . . Though he knows the secrets of more hearts than any other mortal, he is rarely a pessimist. He cares little about paint and powder, warts and wrinkles—the shame and

accidents of life; but looks at the life itself, and sees the man who hides himself even from his own introspection, as he really is. He does not lose faith in human nature, because unexpected acts of heroism and self-sacrifice alternate in his experience with cases of complete atrophy of the moral sense and almost incredible perversion of the right.[28]

And thus the contrived stories describing the legal profession, which Tourgée included in *With Gauge and Swallow* (1889), were feebly justified.

III *Christian Socialism*

But the novel that serves as Tourgée's most impressive statement of humanitarianism is *Murvale Eastman*. On September 17, 1889, his wife recorded in her diary: "After a year and a half of thought, Albion began today his story. The agony—I can use no other word—of decision was intense. He wished to do so well—to put so forcibly the truths which have weighed upon him so long."[29] The novel, which first appeared in a humanitarian magazine *The Advance*, is concerned with the practical application of Christianity in daily living; its hero, Murvale Eastman, "demands that his followers, of all classes and conditions, shall make the welfare of their fellows the first and highest object in life, after their own wants and the comfort of those dependent upon them. This is Christian Socialism."[30]

Eastman, a strong pastor, is violently opposed to "the barons of wealth," those larger manufacturers who have become "more potent in molding the destinies of others than the feudal lords ever were or ever would be";[31] and in his sermons he censures the rich, celebrates the poor, and soon alienates himself from the wealthy members of his congregation. Because of his independent position, he finds himself forcibly opposed by the most important and active church supporter, Wilton Kishu, a man "who never does anything by accident" and who maintains that "the rich man is the prop of civilization and the mainstay of Christianity. He builds the churches, endows the schools, and should be allowed to plunder at will, in order that he may disburse at his own good pleasure."[32]

Eastman, who is at odds with those dominant members of his church, finds it necessary to resign his ministry for a year to consider the practical problems of conducting a life based on Christian Socialism. During a strike of horse-car drivers he laments the abuses that corporation leaders have inflicted on the workers, noticing that "until the recent strike, the company had required its drivers to work from twelve to sixteen hours for a day's work, and had paid the lowest wages at monthly intervals."[33] He disguises himself and, in complete support of the working man, drives a horse car.

This early part of the novel, filled with the resistant, commanding figure of Wilton Kishu; with the underprivileged working people who find it necessary to strike; and with Eastman, who is unyielding in his hostility to "the disease of our time—going on acquiring after we have more than we can use or enjoy,"[34] contains some of Tourgée's finest writing and demonstrates how impressive he can be when he deals with a social or political issue that is of deep personal concern to him. In its concentration on religious hyprocrisy the novel is similar to *The Damnation of Theron Ware* and in its social awareness to *A Hazard of New Fortunes.* Ironically, Tourgée suspends his narrative periodically by chastising Howells and other "realists": "You see the 'realist' is always ready to believe anything mean; but anything decent and manly he declares at once to be unnatural. We, who see life as it is, know that it is just as silly to premise that all men are bad as that all are good."[35] And yet, those scenes in which he describes poverty-stricken people deprived of fair working conditions and Murvale Eastman's own support of the strike are similar in tone though less powerful in their final dramatic effect to the strike scenes in *A Hazard of New Fortunes* and to the abject poverty of the bums in *Sister Carrie.* Tourgée was hardly aware how direct he was in his best fiction and how effective he could be when he was direct.

Like so much of Tourgée's other fiction during this period, *Murvale Eastman* is marred by excessive and unreal intrigue, crime, and sentiment, although here some of the characterization is more dynamic and plausible because of the social theme. Eastman's betrothed is Lilian Kishu, the daughter of Wilton Kishu, who intends to marry the pastor against her father's will. Tourgée uses the girl as an example of the "modern" lover who "believed in love of the old-fashioned, romantic sort, as a thing very pleasant to play in the courting days, but [who] fully accepted the more exalted and reasonable view of later times which is so bluntly expressed by the novelist, Tolstoi . . . when he declares that 'love of the passionate, romantic sort is not to be expected or even desired in marriage.' "[36] Tourgée attempts to picture Lilian Kishu as someone whose romantic standards are not quite ideal enough, and he succeeds in creating a heroine who is reasonably credible: her shame of Eastman when he works along with the laborers, her rejection of him because of his excessive social idealism, and her resentment of her father are all described in valid psychological terms, at times quite powerfully. Tourgée punishes her adequately by marrying her to a rising journalist, one of those to whom "news is the most important element of knowledge, and naughtiness the most important feature of news."[37]

Her father, Wilton Kishu, is more firmly portrayed as the standard villain; and, though his unscrupulous opportunism is too obviously contrasted with Eastman's altruism and selflessness, he emerges nevertheless as a forceful figure, a financial leader of the community who unsuccessfully opposes the movement of Christian Socialism. Kishu's dominance as a church and community leader is impressive, and his moral collapse, caused by the fear that a nefarious past of thievery and alleged kidnapping will be exposed, is moving. But his conversion to Christian Socialism is absurd, and the involved and unlikely excuses for his former evil are disappointing and insipid in a novel so powerfully rooted in credible situations.

Tourgée could not reject the artificial devices of the sentimental novel completely, but in spite of his dependence on lengthy sermons, fortuitous inheritances, disguises, impossible revelations, and the ultimate victory of love and charity, *Murvale Eastman* is a strong indictment of monopolies and those who run them and is written in prose that is suitably aggressive and masculine. With all of its faults the novel has the great redeeming virtue of the author's compassion for the suffering, the maligned, the poverty-stricken. And the moralistic tone throughout the book, so obviously sincere and genuine, is particularly persuasive when Tourgée, like so many other more important and impressive writers of the period, cries out against the evil of class distinctions: "Does God love human degradation? Must the human soul wallow in the mire of vice before he can love or pity it?"[38] With the exception of *A Fool's Errand* and *Bricks Without Straw*, this novel is certainly Tourgée's most impressive work, and one would want to temper only slightly Arthur Hobson Quinn's judgment that it is "the staunchest of [Tourgée's] stories."[39]

IV *Valedictory*

Pactolus Prime, another of Tourgée's novels published in 1890, has a moralistic and homiletic tone similar to that of *Murvale Eastman*. But in this work Tourgée is more adamant and insistent in his social purpose—national education of the Negro—and the book is therefore more static and pedestrian, less readable and dramatic. The novel grows out of Tourgée's active concern with the Negro in 1890. On March 13 he addressed the House Committee on Education and denounced the Blair Educational Bill before Congress at that time; he urged the passage of his own bill, one which advocated the same ideas that had appeared in *An Appeal to Caesar*. The Blair Bill was defeated; and, though Tourgée's counter-proposal was not adopted, he took a further role in urging equal rights for the Negro; on March 21 he spoke in favor of a bill which was intended to protect the voter without regard to race or color; and on March 27, as Mrs. Tourgée reported in her diary, the "first bound copies of 'Pactolus' [were] received," the book that proved to be Tourgée's valedictory to his struggle for the Negro's intellectual freedom.

Pactolus Prime, however, is his least eloquent statement of racial problems; it is a novel of a bitter man, written in bitter language, a novel by a sensitive nationalist, who recognized the complacency of his fellow "citizen-kings" and who would not forget the unfulfilled pledges of the Northern politicians.

It would be convenient for us if this last novel concerning the Negro in America could be considered one of Tourgée's major works, for then it would synthesize his whole career. But *Pactolus Prime* is the product of an author whose literary voice has lost its range and flexibility and power and has become a screeching monotone. We have viewed the steady decline of Tourgée's writing until, now, disquisition, discussion, and debate have become the substance of his tale. Even Joel Chandler Harris, a moderate Southerner, finally grew exasperated with Tourgée's fanaticism. In an article he wrote for the *Atlanta Constitution* he complained that *Pactolus Prime* "is written in the same old vein. The spirit of a wounded savage breathes through it, and each gloomy page makes it appear that in this fair land of the South the ruling race is cold-blooded and cruel, while the blacks are patient martyrs, barred out from their rightful place in society. What shall we say of such a writer? Is he a monomaniac, or simply a refugee from his race?"[40]

In a sense, *Pactolus Prime* is hardly a novel at all; the hero is an unrestrained rebel, a pure Christian, whose cry for freedom pervades the entire book. Pactolus Prime pleads for national aid to education so often that the import of his message is obscured by constant repetition. To him the white man's oppression of the colored man has become exclusively a moral and religious sin, committed "in the name of the white Christ," by men who claim to have "His sanction and approval!"[41] The entire tone of Tourgée's novel is religious. The story proceeds by a series of obvious symbols, until we are lost in a jungle of Gothic terror and religious platitudes, until we have seen the white man upbraided by the irritable Pactolus Prime so often that we find it difficult to sympathize with the Negro any more.

Although Tourgée's moral intention is Christian, his literary devices are modeled on those of the Greek drama; he has used the unity of action, time, place, and the chorus. Furthermore, his protagonist bears a faint resemblance to the Greek tragic hero. In the preface to the novel, the editor tells us that *Pactolus Prime* "is the Edipus of American fiction, not less marked than his classical prototype in the singular pathos of his life, in the patience and hopeless bitterness with which he faces his destiny. . . ."[42]

The narrative begins on Christmas morning; and, as we read, we become aware of and repelled by the factitious symbolic devices: Pactolus Prime is a servile bootblack, a Negro serving the white politicians who visit the "Best Inn"; he is, of course, not the ordinary bootblack, for he is acutely aware of national issues, and when he talks to congressmen, senators, and other men of authority, he impresses them with his perceptive political comments. He shines their shoes on Christmas day, but there is no Christian spirit in the soul of the white man. To Pactolus, Christmas has become a meaningless "holiday." The immediate suffering of the Negro that we witnessed in Tourgée's best work has now become the ranting of a self-pitying man, and the novel remains in our minds as one long tirade against the negligent legislators, against the white America.[43] Pactolus may be patterned after Oedipus, but he has none of the Greek's majesty; he is like a petulant child whose just demands irritate us with their ceaseless reiteration. Tourgée's desire to have the Negro educated became so fervent by the time he wrote *Pactolus Prime* that he could only be impatient with the fictional elements which had once effectively forwarded his message. Pactolus' dialogue (the novel almost becomes a dialogue between him and his white customers) is the dialogue of a partisan politican, not of a fictional character; it is debate, not conversation:

> Money makes a white man, that's true; but even money can't help a 'nigger': he's nothing but a 'nigger', no matter how rich.[44]

> There's one little difficulty 'bout it. Who decided what *was* his [the Negro's] sheer? Who measured it out to him? How did it come to be his sheer? How did he *git* it?[45]

> I think . . . that even a 'nigger' who studies Southern life every day he lives, at first hand and short range, is apt to know more about it than a Northern man who never gets nigh enough to it to *feel* it. There are some things, Senator, that a man can't learn from reports. He must see them, feel them, for himself.[46]

The world of Tourgée's more realistic, more tragic Reconstruction novels seems very far behind us—although the problem presented in *Pactolus Prime* is certainly still pressing—and we realize that this work is only a poor remnant of that world. As Tourgée himself recognized, "When a literary man begins to work over his old 'ads,' by which he won popularity aforetime, he is certainly on the downgrade."[47] And Tourgée's personal decline was caused by the repetition of his fundamental ideas as well as by a decline of literary talent. By the 1890's he found himself holding a distinctly minority point of view. As Paul H. Buck has indicated, the Northerners who attacked the Southern position were few in number: even those most interested in the Negro largely accepted the Southerner's defense.[48] By the late 1890's Tourgée had experienced both political and literary defeat: his proposal of national education as a solution of the Negro's problems was regarded as untenable and his "political documents" were not widely read.[49]

V Waning Talent

Throughout the 1890's Tourgée continued to benefit from the undiscriminating disposition of the reading public; carefully he included the most familiar, threadbare themes and characteristics in his fiction. Fatalism, and the unsuccessful attempt to forestall it, is examined in *A Son of Old Harry* (1892), in which the leading character, Hubert Goodwin, becomes a brigadier-general during the Civil War but is unsuccessful in romance because of his "fate." Tourgée endows his hero with a strong sense of national pride and with the necessary courage and sends him into battle; but the war is only incidentally important and Tourgée burdens the subsequent portions of the novel with excessive melodrama, an eternal triangle, tiresome disquisitions on the need for religion in American society, and a romance that is implausible.

More successful than *A Son of Old Harry* was Tourgée's next novel *Out of the Sunset Sea*, written in 1893. The book, a commercial response to the Chicago World's Fair of 1892, retells the adventures of Christopher Columbus. Better suited to write this kind of novel, Tourgée is close to historical fact and thus able to concentrate on the remarkable feat of Columbus. The English hero of the book, Arthur Lake, sails with Columbus for America; but in the new world he grows greedy for gold and succumbs to the lust that infects other sailors. The novel is filled with the usual sea adventures of historical fiction, and here Tourgée is heavily dependent on Cooper, whom he admired more than any other American novelist—more than any novelist with the exception of Scott. The novel is undistinguished but less implausible than Tourgée's sentimental fiction because of its re-creation of history and certain impressive historical figures.

During these years—from 1885 to 1897—Tourgée was living quietly in the rural community of Mayville, New York, the setting of *Black Ice* and *Button's Inn*, and was contributing sporadic articles to the *Inter Ocean*. It was not until the end of 1894 that his association with this Republican newspaper ended and left him without an organ through which to express his political ideas. He therefore established another journal, *The Basis; A Journal of Citizenship*, in which he espoused the same doctrine of "applied Christianity" that he had demonstrated fictionally in *Murvale Eastman*. The journal was to be "The Basis of Public Peace, Personal Security, Equal Rights, Justice to All, Good Laws, Good Government, National Prosperity, Improved Conditions, AND OF A BETTER WORLD TOMORROW." But it was even less successful than *Our Continent;* by April, 1896, the last issue of the magazine was published.

At the same time Tourgée was busy writing another ill-fated sentimental novel, *The Mortgage on the Hip-Roof House* (1896), a short work in which the Horatio Alger myth is unabashedly recounted. The central problem of the novel is the mortgage that must be paid; and, as might be expected, the young hero, an adopted grandson, helps his poverty-stricken grandfather with his debt and wins the admiration and eventual love of the granddaughter. The scene is once again Tourgée's neighborhood of Mayville, near Lake Erie; the plot is mechanical and uninteresting—we can even sense Tourgée's own lack of interest in what he is writing—but there is a pathetic quality that grows out of Tourgée's concentration on the poverty of this family. His fiction has always had the unmistakable quality of autobiography, and here it is the tone of despair that affects the reader.

During the fall of 1896—after he had completed *The Mortgage of the Hip-Roof House*—Tourgée went to New York in an attempt to publish several articles he had written and to campaign for McKinley. Often during these months he wrote to his wife threatening suicide if he could not find some greater financial stability than that which he was realizing through his writings. He was making little money from his published fiction, and he could find no journals that would publish his essays. By December 31, 1896, Emma Tourgée was able to record in her diary, "The close of the most distressful year of my life! Pray God the next may be different."

In 1897 Tourgée was fortunate enough to be appointed consul at Bordeaux because of the many speeches he had made for McKinley during the 1896 presidential campaign. On July 3, 1897, he sailed for France with his wife and daughter, arriving at Bordeaux on August 2. During these last years of his life, Tourgée was periodically ill, not only from old war wounds, but from diabetes as well, a disease which caused a constant loss of strength until his death in 1905. His writings, few and unimpressive, were final gestures that never proved wholly successful. In 1898 he published *The Man Who Outlived Him-*

self, a collection of three short novels—the title story, *Poor Joel Pike,* and *The Grave of Tante Angelique.*

The Man Who Outlived Himself is depressing to read, not because of its limitations as a work of art but because of the weariness, sorrow, and hopelessness with which the book is written. The novel was inspired by Tourgée's sense of his own failure as a businessman, writer, and politician—failure indeed is the theme of the novel. Philip Devens, Tourgée's hero and alter ego, has lost his fortune in Wall Street and is overwhelmingly dejected. He has concluded "that the chief element of success in the world is not genius, nor cleverness, nor intellectual capacity of any sort, but simply an intuitive faculty of determining just the right time to let go. Doggedness is a common enough virtue, if it be a virtue, but the ability to know when to stop is a divine gift. 'The final perseverance of the saints' may be a good theological dogma, but I have noticed that most of those who practice it, as regards earthly affairs, at least, die poor."[50] The novel is written in this style, not passionate or tendentious, but quietly satirical, even urbane; it indicates—like so many of Tourgée's poorer fictions—that however poor the various aspects of any particular novel, Tourgée's prose is consistently readable.

In the midst of his financial difficulties, Devens dies, comes back to life, and discovers himself in a mental institution. He begins to realize that he has been a victim of amnesia and, as he recovers his memory, he makes his way to New York to live a new life. In the ten years that have elapsed since his death, the customs of America have changed, especially those of women. "To look at them upon the street or in the cars," Tourgée observes, "it seems as if the old relation was changing, and the women coming to be the larger and the stronger type."[51] From a former friend Devens learns that his wife is alive and prosperous and that under her guidance their stock has risen in value during his absence. The two of course are united happily, in spite of the fact that Devens regrets his wife's independent success.

The Man Who Outlived Himself is a revealing expression of the condition of Tourgée's own marriage, which was strained many times by Tourgée's uncertain business ventures. His wife was infinitely patient with his vacillating, impracticable nature, and as Roy F. Dibble has suggested, hardly failed through these years of trial and continual disappointment to be his constant inspiration; while, in a more practical sense, it was largely due to her untiring energy, despite frequent attacks of illness which often overcame her, that Tourgée's literary and business ventures attained what small success they did. Without her assistance in the office as amanuensis, proof-reader and general business manager, their financial condition would have been much worse, and the retention of Thoreim, the maintenance of which cost no little sum on account of its large size, would have been impossible. Besides this constant fear of financial ruin, she had to bear with the many irritable traits of her husband. His headstrong nature, his cocksure confidence in his own opinions, his excessive love of fishing with the accompanying waste of many valuable days, his constant desire to enter the political arena—all these well-defined traits of his taxed her wifely powers of diplomacy to the uttermost.[52]

Tourgée was fully aware of his limitations, and in later life—as *The Man Who Outlived Himself* testifies—he became even morbidly self-deprecatory.

In the second short novel, *Poor Joel Pike,* Tourgée draws upon his legal experience; and, like those stories included in *With Gauge and Swallow,* this small work combines suspense and sentiment, humor and morality. Joel Pike is a comic character, a hermit and an old codger reminiscent of Dominicus Pike in Hawthorne's story, "Mr. Higginbotham's Catastrophe." Pike comes to the firm of Harmon and Ruggles and, as he tells Ruggles his tale of intrigue, we learn that he was in love with Susan Gedney Harrington and, rebuffed by the old woman, has fallen in love with her daughter. We also learn that there has been a long-time enmity between Harrington and himself, that he owns the old Gedney place, and that he has been accused of assault and battery for "hitting" the Gedney daughter when she jilted him and threatened to run away with a young man. This novel, so dependent on the artificial techniques of sentimental and Gothic fiction, ends in the expected manner: Pike reveals that he had been helping to support Sadie Harrington and her mother since the death of the father, a "dissolute vagabond." Thus the misjudged old codger is really genial and beneficent, bestowing his generosity on less fortunate people.

The last of the novels included in *The Man Who Outlived*

Himself is entitled *The Grave of Tante Angelique*. It is the poorest of the three works in spite of the fact that Tourgée returns to the South for his setting, for here history is unimportant and locale only vaguely realized. The hero is a Northern stonecutter who travels South for business and prevents the villain, Colonel Archie Dinsemer, from inheriting wealth that rightfully belongs to Eloise, the daughter of his dead sister, Angelique. Tourgée's protagonist falls in love with Eloise and together they help reform the villain; they succeed, in part, by presenting him with half the inheritance. This little novel, which has curious similarities to Cable's "DesMoiselles Plantation," is burdened by the too familiar motive of sentimental heroism that we have noticed in *Figs and Thistles, Black Ice, Button's Inn,* and other works—the poor Northern boy prospers through industry, self-reliance, and morality, becomes a senator and a millionaire, and marries the heroine.

CHAPTER 8

The Wisdom of Folly

THE LAST YEARS of Tourgée's life were spent in relative obscurity as a consul in Bordeaux. He published little during this period, and the few short articles that were finally printed—one commenting on the mores of Europe, another on the consular system, a third offering advice to young voters[1]—gained little attention even from the audience he had once attracted. His most interesting writing at this time is his private correspondence; in it he takes account of his views—particularly regarding the Negro—and measures their validity in painfully honest historical terms.

Throughout the 1880's and 1890's Tourgée had continually reminded the Northerner of his responsibility to the Negro. But, as he came to realize, his ceaseless censures had fallen upon deaf ears: Northern Republicans and Democrats, as Rayford W. Logan has shown, had been in the process of deserting the Negro. At the end of his administration, Hayes had left "white supremacy . . . more securely entrenched in the South" than when he had entered the White House; and "Presidents Garfield, Arthur and Cleveland allowed the Southern question to simmer during the next eight years, 1881-1889."[2] It had become evident by the end of Cleveland's first administration that "presidents of both parties uttered pious platitudes but said nothing and did nothing except to give a few jobs to professional Negro officeholders."[3]

Tourgée was fighting fictionally wars which had already been fought in the 1870's: he was presenting his vivid, persuasive interpretation of Reconstruction problems so that Northerners would realize the need of *his* answers for the neglected Negro. But he was addressing a minority of Northerners in magazines and newspapers which did not represent the attitude of the general public. During President Hayes's administration "The Northern press, on the whole, wanted Negroes to remain in the South"—political commentators considered the Negro problem a Southern problem—and "by 1886 most Northerners were infernally tired of hearing about the Negro question."[4] In brief, "the Northern press was not too reluctant to sacrifice the Negro on the altar of reconciliation, peace and prosperity."[5]

In the last years of his life, Tourgée lost faith in his own educational theories. He felt that even education would not help to improve the status of the Negro. On October 21, 1901, he wrote to President Theodore Roosevelt congratulating him for being courageous enough to invite Booker T. Washington to dinner—in spite of the violent protests of Southerners—and then offered one of his last comments on the issue of national education as a solution to the Negro problem: "It was a genuine fool's notion. I sincerely believed at that time (1880) that education and Christianity were infallible solvents of all the evils which have resulted from the white man's claim of individual superiority. . . . Today I am ashamed to have been that sort of a fool. I realize now that . . . education does not eradicate prejudice, but intensifies it—Christianity does not condemn or prevent injustice done to the weak by the strong, but encourages and excuses it."[6] In any civilization where there are white and Negro people living together, he wrote to a friend in 1902, there will always be a dominant race; and in America that dominant race will always be white. "Education," he continued in this same letter, will "do anything for the colored people except to make him more sensible of his wrongs and render him desperate in his longings to ameliorate the evils which beset him."[7]

This pessimistic attitude stemmed from a lifetime of political failure. Unable as a practical politician to promote his humanitarian reforms for the Negro, Tourgée became a professional novelist who wrote political fiction which also proved ineffective in achieving his idealistic goals. Tourgée realized that Southern authors were victorious in creating the lasting impression of Reconstruction; they succeeded, he wrote in 1888, in convincing the American reading public that the carpetbaggers had misused the Southern people and had falsified the picture of social and political difficulties which had attended "the tragic era."[8]

Rather than accept the fact that racial equality could be

realized only after a long period of time, Tourgée was certain, towards the end of his life, that the Negro would never be granted justice. Bitterly he recorded his extreme disillusionment in the political leaders and people of his time who, as he believed, had "substituted caste for slavery."

I have learned something since I wrote "A Fool's Errand." I believed in many things then, such as the Fatherhood of God and the brotherhood of Man. I believed in Christianity (the modern article measured and prescribed by those who know and declare its function). I believed in the U. S. and the flower of liberty, security and equal right for all. I believed the abolition of Slavery was all that was required to establish security before the law. I was so proud of our government and civilization that I could not endure the thought that it should be stained with injustice and oppression. I believed in that curious fetich of our modern thought "Education" as a remedy for wrong. When I wrote "The remedy for Wrong is Righteousness; for Darkness, Light. Make the spelling-book the scepter of national power!"— I believed every word of this Fool's Gospel.

Now I realize its folly, though I am glad that I then believed. Now, I realize the terrible truth that neither Education, Christianity, nor Civilization, mean justice or equality between man and man, when one is white and the other colored. White Christianity twists with enthusiasm the Master's words to excuse wrong to the colored man individually and collectively. There has never been a white Christian people who were willing to give a colored people equal opportunity, equal right and security to enjoy "life, liberty and the pursuit of happiness." Even our American Christian slavery was the worst ever known on earth. . . . Unless God intervenes there is no other fate before the colored American whom the Nation made a citizen but whom neither the courts nor Christian sentiment will grant protection in his rights as a man or as a citizen. . . .

It is the very highest form of blasphemy to claim that the idea of "white supremacy" and the later barbarism which demands race-subjection or extermination is pleasing to God or conformable to the religion of the Man of Nazareth. Modern Christianity shuts its eyes because these things are done by white Christians in its name, and those who suffer are colored peoples in whom the Church has no interest except in their salvation. We are willing to furnish them with unlimited promises of heavenly delights, but not willing to accord them equal rights and opportunities on earth.

It is because of this ineradicable and almost universal attribute
of the Southern whites that neither education nor Christianity
nor both combined offer the slightest hope for the solution of
this problem—a problem the most important by all odds, that
Civilization and Christianity have been called upon to face. If
Civilization and Christianity cannot furnish a public opinion—a
general impulse—which will compel the Southern whites to loosen
the grip they are tightening year by year on the manhood and
equal rights of the colored American, Christianity will certainly
lose its hold upon humanity as a religion of Justice and Truth—
let alone all consideration of the love it boasts to have for others.[9]

Tourgée was never able to view the South with dispassionate
eyes, for he had worked tirelessly to secure equal rights for the
Negro, and he had failed. He almost always spoke of his "fool's
errand" as representing the abortive attempt of all carpetbaggers to improve Southern conditions; but the animosity of
North Carolinians, the defeat he suffered as a Congressional
candidate, the Southern opposition which he encountered at
various state conventions, and the public indifference to his
proposals for national education made him excessively bitter in
a very personal way.

Tourgée felt that his mission to North Carolina had been a
"fool's errand," but he did not recognize until the end of his
life just how small his sympathetic audience had grown. Obdurate
as always, he desired, upon his return to New York in 1879, to
convince Northerners of the urgency of national education for
Southern Negroes and whites: that was the issue at the center
of his Reconstruction novels. Tourgée was different from most
popular writers in that his political beliefs were of far greater
importance than the novel or story that included them; unlike
Harris, Page, and other writers, he was not content to describe
local folkways and traditions, nor was he able to relate a story
for its own sake alone. His fictions are fundamentally political
tracts, and any analysis of them—as has been suggested—must
be firmly based on the knowledge that they are significant as
social criticism and not as literary art.

Yet, with all his limitations as novelist—his melodrama, occa-
sional rhetoric, idealized types, his contrived situations, lack of
humor, and tendency to sermonize—Tourgée is certainly one of
the most vigorous and exciting writers who have described the
post-bellum South. He has a style that is commanding and

assertive, a fit instrument for the vivid material he presents in his best novels; he has an insight into the conditions of Reconstruction that is penetrating because of his singular position as an informed, sensitive, and forthright Northerner in the South; and he conveys his ideas with a moral and humane fervor so obviously sincere that, like those Southerners who opposed him politically, one is compelled to admire him. As Edmund Wilson has suggested, "Tourgée is one of the most readable in this second category of writers who aim primarily at social history. His narrative has spirit and movement; his insights are brilliantly revealing, and they are expressed with emotional conviction."[10]

Tourgée considered himself in alliance with those "brilliant" writers like E. P. Roe and F. Marion Crawford who were clarifying the complex historical issues of his day. In terms of literature as well as politics he admired only those authors whose beliefs corroborated his own—Cooper, Hawthorne, and the lesser known E. P. Roe and Helen Hunt Jackson. The English Victorian novelists were also the objects of his adulation, and the morality, so organically essential to the fiction of George Eliot and Charles Reade, Tourgée feebly emulated. Of Reade, Tourgée wrote: "He recognized the underlying truth of all artistic production, that its highest purpose is to teach a noble lesson."[11]

Tourgée attempted to teach—indeed we might say to preach—his own version of a "noble lesson," but he provided himself with an unpopular text, and his lecture was quite different from that of other authors describing the Reconstruction South. Tourgée was politically out of step with his contemporaries—not only with the majority of politicians but with literary men as well. Written at a time when Northerners were losing interest in the Negro, *A Fool's Errand* and *Bricks Without Straw* proved popular because they were the only complete fictional accounts of Reconstruction until that time; and the public was extremely curious regarding the conditions that had existed in the South. But it was curiosity rather than sympathy that had led people to read Tourgée's best novels. When that interest had been satisfied by subsequent writers—writers who described the South in a more conciliatory and hence more agreeable fashion—the general response to Tourgée was one of hostility or, at best, of indifference.

Tourgée's fiction is the literary *apologia* of Radical Republicanism; as such it clarifies a political position few Reconstruction authors were willing or qualified to understand. Thomas Nelson Page, Joel Chandler Harris, and Thomas Dixon, the leading exponents of the Southern point of view, were all quite young during Reconstruction. When they wrote their novels of Reconstruction at the turn of the century, they were recalling boyhood memories that surely must have faded in the decades that had elapsed since the 1860's and 1870's. Moreover, these authors used journalistic accounts which were unreliable and exaggerated in their treatment of Radical Republicanism. The works of Page, Harris, and Dixon perpetuate a bias which was first recorded in the newspapers of the period; and we have seen, in our discussion of Tourgée as a carpetbagger, how misleading the journalism of the period can be.

Of all those authors who fictionalized the Reconstruction era, Tourgée was the only one who lived in the South as an adult throughout the entire period, the only one who offered a first-hand account of Reconstruction in terms of the political, social, and economic conflicts between Southerners and Radical Republicans. His political experiences are transcribed into writing that is personally moving and historically perceptive; his best work, unlike that of other Reconstruction authors, is a contemporaneous, vital testament of Reconstruction in the South. In any discussion of post-bellum popular literature, novels like *A Fool's Errand* and *Bricks Without Straw* are worth consideration, for nowhere else in the history of American letters are the experiences of a carpetbagger reported so comprehensively.

Notes and References

Preface

1. George J. Becker, "Albion W. Tourgée: Pioneer in Social Criticism," *American Literature,* XIX (March, 1947), 59.

Chapter One

1. Roy F. Dibble, *Albion W. Tourgée* (New York, 1921), p. 16.
2. *Ibid.,* p. 15.
3. *Ibid.,* p. 17.
4. Tourgée to Emma Kilbourne (the woman whom he married on May 14, 1863), February 4, 1860.
5. Asahel C. Kendrick, *Martin B. Anderson, LL.D. A Biography* (Philadelphia, 1895), pp. 286-87.
6. Later, on May 2, 1864, Tourgée "was admitted to the bar at Painsville, Ohio, and at once entered the law office of . . . Sherman & Farmer. On July 2, licenses to practice law and to act as Claims Agent were granted him at Ashtabula, Ohio" (Dibble, pp. 30-31).
7. *Ibid.,* p. 29. See also William W. Williams, *History of Ashtabula County, Ohio, With Illustrations of Its Pioneers and Most Prominent Men* (Philadelphia, 1878), p. 53. Later in his life Tourgée recorded the activities of this unit in a book called *The Story of a Thousand* (New York, 1896).
8. Tourgée, "The Christian Citizen," *The Chautauquan,* II (November, 1881), 90.
9. War Diary entry, June 22, 1863.
10. Jonathan Worth to Giles Mebane, January 7, 1868; Jonathan Worth, *The Correspondence of Jonathan Worth,* ed. J. G. de Roulhac Hamilton (Raleigh, 1909), II, 1119.
11. W. W. Holden to Tourgée, June 16, 1865. Holden was appointed provisional governor by President Johnson, a native North Carolinian, on May 29, 1865, and was relieved of his duties on December 23, 1865. In the gubernatorial election, held on November 9, 1865, Holden lost to Jonathan Worth, who remained governor until November, 1868.
12. Albion W. Tourgée, *A Fool's Errand* (New York, 1879), p. 3.
13. On March 16, 1866, "a firm was organized by Tourgée, Seneca Kuhn of Greensboro, and R. L. Pettingill, formerly of Rochester, with a joint capital of $4500 in three equal shares, to be known as the Tourgée, Kuhn & Pettingill Firm, for the purpose of conducting the nursery business." But "Pettingill withdrew from the nursery firm

in the following summer, and Kuhn followed suit on December, 1866." In June, 1867, Tourgée found himself several thousand dollars in debt" (Dibble, pp. 34-35).

When he became a judge in 1868, Tourgée was able to repay his outstanding debts, but in 1871 he once again entered the business world. He formed the North Carolina Handle Company, having conceived the idea that some of the timber in the state might be converted into various types of tool-handles. Once again he was unsuccessful, and his liabilities amounted to $30,000. These debts he repaid from the sales of his novels, his work as pension agent in Raleigh, North Carolina, and lecturing. By June 20, 1876, he was able to write a friend: "The monetary misfortunes of which you are already informed have given me two years of very hard work, though I can now see that they have been of great advantage to me."

14. Tourgée, *The Story of a Thousand* (Buffalo, 1896), p. 72.

15. John T. Trowbridge, *The South; a Tour of its Battlefields and Ruined Cities, A Journey Through the Desolated States, and Talks with the People* (Hartford, 1866), p. 586.

16. Sidney Andrews, *The South Since the War as Shown by Fourteen Weeks of Travel and Observations in Georgia and the Carolinas* (Boston, 1866), p. 384. See also Whitelaw Reid, *After the War; a Southern Tour, May 1, 1865, To May 1, 1866* (New York, 1866), p. 598, and Thomas W. Knox, *Campfire and Cottonfield* (New York, 1866), p. 496.

As the Reconstruction measures of the Radical Republicans exerted a notably pernicious effect on the South in the 1870's, another attitude—far more sympathetic to the South—became apparent from the observations of certain Northern travelers. See as typical of this later point of view Edward King, *The Great South* (New York, 1875), pp. i-ii; James S. Pike, *The Prostrate State, South Carolina Under Negro Government* (New York, 1935), p. 12; Charles Nordhoff, *The Cotton States in the Spring and Summer of 1875* (New York, 1876), p. 108; Edwin DeLeon, "The New South," *Harper's Monthly Magazine*, XLVIII (January, 1874), 270-80, XLVIII (February, 1874), 406-22, XLIX (September, 1874), 555-68.

The general tendency on the part of most journalists in the 1870's was to avoid any issue which might lead to renewed hostility between North and South. The evils of Reconstruction were not overlooked, but they were considered temporary. Tourgée was out of step with his contemporaries; unlike other writers of the time, he refused to acknowledge that readers were no longer interested in contentious articles and books describing a barbarous South.

17. Trowbridge, p. 502.

18. Andrews, p. 4.

19. E. Merton Coulter, *The South During Reconstruction, 1865-1877* (Baton Rouge, 1947), p. 24.

20. *The Union Register,* January 3, 1867. Tourgée was editor of this newspaper from January 3, 1867-June 14, 1867.

21. *Ibid.,* June 14, 1867.

22. Henderson H. Donald, *The Negro Freedman, Life Conditions of the American Negro in the Early Years After Emancipation* (New York, 1952), pp. 200-25 *passim.*

23. Horace W. Raper, "William W. Holden and the Peace Movement' in North Carolina," *The North Carolina Historical Review,* XXXI (October, 1954), 493-516 *passim;* Georgia Lee Tatum, *Disloyalty in the Confederacy* (Chapel Hill, 1934), pp. 111-15, 128-33.

24. Manuscript notebook, 1866.

25. J. G. de Roulhac Hamilton, *Reconstruction in North Carolina* (New York, 1914), p. 181.

26. *Ibid.,* pp. 187-88.

27. Tourgée, *A Fool's Errand,* p. 115.

28. Quoted in *Raleigh Daily Sentinel,* April 29, 1867.

29. *Raleigh Daily North Carolina Standard,* January 12, February 15, 1867.

30. *Raleigh Daily Sentinel,* February 12, 1867.

31. *The Greensboro Patriot,* December 11, 1867.

32. *Raleigh Daily Sentinel,* April 12, 1867.

33. W. Dunn, Jr. to A. B. Chapin [co-editor of *The Union Register*], April 20, 1867.

34. Hamilton, p. 336.

35. J. M. Edmunds to Tourgée, March 3, 1867.

36. Document is dated April, 1867, and signed "Appointed by Grand Council," Chief, J. M. Edmunds, Washington, D. C.

37. *Raleigh Daily North Carolina Standard,* May 21, 23, 1867.

38. J. R. Bulla to Tourgée, August 7, 1868. Bulla was the prosecutor for the courts of which Tourgée was judge.

39. *The New York Tribune,* April 4, 1881, p. 5.

40. *The New York Herald,* September 8, 1866, p. 1.

41. Samuel A. Court Ashe, History of North Carolina, II (Raleigh, 1925), 925. Josiah Turner, conservative editor of the *Raleigh Daily Sentinel,* said in his testimony at the Ku Klux hearings that he "offered one hundred dollars in gold if any black man could get Tourgée to name the respectable Quaker that told him so." *Reports of the Committees of the Senate of the United States for the Second Session of the Forty-Second Congress, 1771-'72,* I (Washington, 1872), 376. This document will hereafter be called *Senate Report.*

Governor Worth wrote a North Carolinian who sat in the convention that sent Tourgée as a delegate, demanding the names of the twelve hundred men and the location of the pond where the fifteen murdered Negroes had been found. Jonathan Worth, *The Correspondence of Jonathan Worth*, coll. and ed. J. G. de Roulhac Hamilton, II (Raleigh, 1909), 773-74.

42. *The New York Herald*, September 8, 1866, p. 1. Tourgée was only one of many Radicals who vilified Johnson and Southern conservatives. See Howard K. Beale, *The Critical Year: A Study of Andrew Johnson and Reconstruction* (New York, 1930), pp. 269-71. Tourgée is using his "Quaker source" as a direct appeal to the residents of the Quaker city, Philadelphia; the *argumentum ad hominem* seems patent. In addition, Guilford was "the center of the influence and strength of the Society of Friends in North Carolina"; Tourgée is also appealing to the Quakers of North Carolina. Sallie W. Stockard, *The History of Guilford County* (Knoxville, Tennessee, 1902), p. 123.

43. Worth to Nereus Mendenhall, September 10, 1866, *Worth Correspondence*, II, 773. Worth goes on to specify exactly what petitions had been referred to him by the president. In a letter to the editor of *The Greensboro Patriot*, September 10, 1866, he challenged Tourgée to "vindicate his facts," and suggested that the leading Quakers of North Carolina "disabuse themselves and the Quakers of North Carolina from endorsing Tourgée's iniquitious lies." Tourgée never proved the statements. On May 22, 1875, he wrote to Joseph C. Abbott, the editor of the *Wilmington Post*, that the Quaker "who told me is still living in this county and is willing to state upon oath at any time that he made the statement to me in the presence of two others. Whether it is true or not I do not know or care. I told it as 'twas told to me."

44. Manuscript notes for a speech delivered in Pennsylvania, fall of 1866.

45. Anonymous letter to Tourgée, September 24, 1866.

46. Anonymous letter to Tourgée's wife, October 16, 1866.

47. Tourgée to his wife, September 16, 1866.

48. William Archibald Dunning, *Reconstruction Political and Economic* (New York, 1907), p. 93.

49. See letter to Thaddeus Stevens by W. F. Henderson, H. Adams, George Kinney, P. A. Long, George Riley, in James A. Padgett, "Reconstruction Letters from North Carolina," *The North Carolina Historical Review*, XXI (July, 1944), 242-44.

50. Tourgée, *Bricks Without Straw* (New York, 1880), p. 400.

51. *Idem.*

52. Hamilton, p. 366.

53. Hugh Talmage Lefler (ed.), *North Carolina History Told by Contemporaries* (Chapel Hill, 1934), p. 334.

54. Hugh T. Lefler and Albert Newsome, *The History of a Southern State North Carolina* (Chapel Hill, 1954), p. 460.

55. Tourgée to his daughter, February 1, 1890.

56. Quoted in Hamilton, p. 263. See also *Journal of Constitutional Convention of 1868*, pp. 141-42, where Tourgée expresses further concern about the state debt.

57. Hugh T. Lefler and Albert Newsome, *History of North Carolina*, p. 461.

58. *Constitution of 1868*, pp. 7, 27, 28, 29, 31.

59. William A. Devin, "Footprints of a Carpetbagger," *The Torch*, XVII (April, 1944), 18.

60. Tourgée, *A Fool's Errand*, p. 141.

61. Worth to Giles Mebane, January 7, 1868, *Worth Correspondence*, II, 1119.

62. Worth to E. A. Jones, January 7, 1868; *ibid.*, p. 1120.

63. Worth to D. F. Caldwell, R. P. McLean, and R. Gorrell, January 6, 1868, *ibid.*, p. 1114.

64. Worth to D. F. Caldwell, R. P. McLean, and R. Gorrell, January 6, 1868; *ibid.*, pp. 1114-19, *passim.* Worth quotes from Canby's letter. Holden had recommended Tourgée to General Canby for the appointment (see *National Anti-Slavery Standard*, December 14, 1867), but Worth objected to his moral character. Those people to whom Worth is writing are citizens of North Carolina.

65. Worth to B. S. Hendrick, January 8, 1868, *Worth Correspondence*, p. 1123.

66. Hamilton, pp. 286-87, notes that "the Republicans polled almost their full strength," whereas the "large number of Conservatives, qualified to vote, failed to do so. This was, in part, the result of the general belief that, if the Conservatives were successful, Congress would set aside the election or refuse to remove the disabilities of those Conservatives who were elected to office."

67. Tourgée to Republican State Committee, March 21, 1868.

68. Tourgée to Lucy J. Rider, March 2, 1869.

69. William A. Devin, "Footprints of a Carpetbagger," p. 19. Devin has been Chief Justice of the Supreme Court of North Carolina since 1951. The requirements of the present study forbid any extended and detailed documentation of the contention that Tourgée was an able, impartial, and honest judge. A close examination of his role as a judge is provided in the present writer's *Albion W. Tourgée: Reporter of the Reconstruction*, unpublished Ph.D. dissertation, Columbia University, 1960, pp. 32-51.

70. Tourgée, *The Code of Civil Procedure of North Carolina with Notes and Decisions* (Raleigh, 1878), p. i.

71. J. M. McCorkle to Tourgée, August 25, 1879.

72. Devin, "Footprints of a Carpetbagger," p. 18.

73. W. H. Smith, Thos. Sitch, John H. Dillard, justices, to Tourgée, August 22, 1879.

74. George Washington Brooks to Tourgée, September 12, 1879; Charles Price to Tourgée, August 2, 1873; W. H. Bailey to Tourgée, August 25, 1879; Frederick Philips to Tourgée, July 18, 1878; Ang. F. Seymour to Tourgée [undated]; D. L. Rippell to Tourgée, October, 1879; E. C. Graham to Tourgée, August 26, 1879; J. R. B. Burchard to Tourgée, August 27, 1879.

After Tourgée's death on May 21, 1905, many obituaries appeared in Northern and Southern newspapers. One article, written by a Southerner, received high praise from William Busbey, editor at that time of the Chicago *Inter Ocean*. On September 14, 1905, Busbey wrote to Mrs. D. K. Hall: "I return the article of Judge Tourgée from the Raleigh News Observer. I agree with you that it is one of the very best called out by the death of Judge Tourgée. I do not know the writer, but evidently he knew the judge and followed his career with interest and sympathy. All that he says as the feelings of North Carolinians to the Judge is borne out by what Charles Busbee, a prominent lawyer of Raleigh, said to me several years ago. Busbee spoke in the same enthusiastic terms of the civil code and of Judge Tourgée's fairness on the bench."

75. John Manning to Tourgée, October 20, 1879. Hamilton, p. 415, notes that "a number of able lawyers, who were his political opponents, have assured the writer that Tourgée was the ablest judge that they had ever practiced under."

76. "Emancipation—considered as an historical event" and "Next Crusade" are undated speeches, but the envelope containing these manuscripts is marked "Addresses to Negroes when he was a judge—n/date."

77. Tourgée, while serving as judge, recorded many of the sworn testimonials of Negroes who had been victimized by the Ku Klux Klan. These testimonials form the substance of *The Invisible Empire*. One distinction should be made between Harriet Beecher Stowe's *A Key* and Tourgée's *Invisible Empire*: whereas "practically every item in the Key was sought out *ad hoc* after Uncle Tom was finished," (J. C. Furnas, *Goodbye to Uncle Tom* [New York, 1956], p. 27) Tourgée's information had been compiled before *A Fool's Errand* was written.

78. Stanley F. Horn, *Invisible Empire, The Story of the Ku Klux Klan, 1866-1871* (Boston, 1939), p. 195.

79. C. Alphonso Smith, *O. Henry Biography* (New York, 1916), p. 61.

80. Quoted in *ibid.*, p. 66. Tourgée's reputation suffered greatly because of his activities at the 1868 state convention. As a Republican leader, he was considered partially responsible for the unnecessary expense of the convention. His extravagance was borne out by his favoring a high *per diem* rate for members at the convention; his attempt to "wreck . . . the financial integrity" of North Carolina was indicated, Southerners felt, by his desire to have the entire state debt repudiated.

Tourgée was never "the Republican boss of the state," though people living in Guilford County thought of him as a powerful leader of the Radical party, second in authority to Holden. He was Holden's underling, though not so powerful as his vociferous denunciations of the South made North Carolinians believe.

81. "After seventy ballots, W. F. Henderson was chosen. . . . Tourgée soon after reached the conclusion that Reconstruction was 'an ignominious failure,' an opinion he held for some years until a pension agency made him see a brighter side" (Hamilton, p. 601).

82. Dibble, p. 47.

83. Quoted in *ibid.*, p. 41.

Chapter Two

1. Tourgée, *A Royal Gentleman* (New York, 1881), p. iii.

2. Dibble, p. 32.

3. The character of 'Toinette, for example, is based on the daughter of Tourgée's cook, a girl named Addie. Tourgée offered the young mulatto an education and treated her as one of the family. She traveled to the North, and people assumed she was white; soon, however, she returned to Greensboro and became an established and respected member of the community. Addie to Tourgée, July 18, 1875.

4. Trowbridge, *My Own Story* (New York, 1903), pp. 310-11.

5. Tourgée, *A Royal Gentleman*, p. v.

6. John W. De Forest, *A Union Officer in the Reconstruction* (New Haven, 1948), pp. 193, 703-4.

7. Jay B. Hubbell, "Some New Letters of Constance Fenimore Woolson," *New England Quarterly*, XIV (December, 1941), 722.

8. Francis P. Gaines, *The Southern Plantation: A Study in the Development and the Accuracy of a Tradition* (New York, 1924), pp. 68-69.

9. Edmund Wilson, *Patriotic Gore: Studies in the Literature of the American Civil War* (New York, 1962), p. 533.

10. Tourgée, *A Royal Gentleman*, p. 24.

11. Tourgée abides by this standard distinction between the mulatto and the pure-bred Negro, a distinction that held true in the post-

Civil War period as well as in ante-bellum times. All of Tourgée's insurgent Negroes are mulattoes.

12. Tourgée, *A Royal Gentleman*, p. 78.

13. J. C. Furnas, in his *Goodbye to Uncle Tom* (New York, 1956), cites many cases of plantation owners who had colored girls as concubines (see pp. 135-49 *passim*). The fact that 'Toinette is mulatto and so light colored that she can be hardly distinguished from a white girl makes her all the more desirable. But despite the fact that Geoffrey Hunter is engaged in interbreeding himself, he naturally cannot accept 'Toinette as his wife before or after she has attained freedom.

14. Tourgée, *A Royal Gentleman*, p. 242.

15. *Ibid.*, pp. 377-78.

16. *Ibid.*, p. v.

17. Tourgée to E. H. Johnson, May 15, 1902.

18. Tourgée to his wife, January 5, 1873.

19. Lincoln, to Tourgée, was the greatest spiritual leader the human race had encountered since Christ. His description in *A Royal Gentleman*, p. 395, is typical: "Others may have been greater in gifts and learning, in intellect and will, more brilliant in action, more fertile in resource, more varied in accomplishment, more commanding in power:—but in the glory of high and bold purpose, faithfully, trustfully, and tenderly fulfilled; of a transcendent mission executed with unwearying humility and zeal, Abraham Lincoln stands the first among the men whom the ages have brought forth—that man who walked 'with firmness in the right, as God gives us to see the right'—'with malice toward none, and with charity for all.' "

20. *Ibid.*, p. 441.

21. Charles Hampton Nilon, *Some Aspects of the Treatment of Negro Character by Five Representative American Novelists: Cooper, Melville, Tourgée, Glasgow, Faulkner* (unpublished Ph.D. dissertation, University of Wisconsin, 1952), p. 124.

22. Tourgée, *A Royal Gentleman*, pp. v-vi.

23. De Forest suggested such a relationship in "A Gentleman of the Old School," *The Atlantic Monthly*, XXI (May, 1868), 546-55. But in this story the author concentrates on the South Carolina gentleman and his kind treatment of his slaves, who happen to be also his children. Mary Louise Pool, in "Told by an Octoroon," *Galaxy*, X (December, 1870), 827-38, deals with this problem more directly.

The theme of miscegenation was vastly popular. In Mark Twain's *Pudd'nhead Wilson* and Constance Fenimore Woolson's "Jeanette" (1886) the unhappy consequences of mixed blood are explored. Matt Crim, in "Was It an Exceptional Case" (1891), describes the loss of affection a Northern lover experiences when he discovers that his wife has Negroid blood. Variations of the motive are to be found in Dion Boucicault's play *The Octoroon* (1859), Sherwood Bonner's "A Volcanic Interlude" (1880), Alice I. Jones's *Beatrice of Bayou Têche* (1895), William N. Harben's *White Marie* (1889), Joel C. Harris' "Where's Duncan?", Kate Chopin's "Desiree's Baby" (1893), and W. E. B. Dubois's *Darkwater* (1920).

24. *The Charlotte Observer*, September 12, 1874.

25. *Journal of 1875 Convention*, p. 264.

26. Tourgée, *A Royal Gentleman*, p. v.

27. Wilson, p. 534.

28. Tourgée, *A Royal Gentleman*, p. v.

29. Shields McIlwaine, *The Southern Poor-White from Lubberland to Tobacco Road* (Norman, Oklahoma, 1939), p. 88.

30. De Forest, *A Union Officer in the Reconstruction*, p. 158. See De Forest's story, "An Independent Ku Klux," *Galaxy*, XIII (April, 1872), 480-88 for his finest characterization of the poor white, Selnarten Bowen. Other depictions of the poor white are Randolph Armitage and Nancy Gile in *Kate Beaumont*.

31. Constance Fenimore Woolson, "King David," *Rodman the Keeper. Southern Sketches* (New York, 1879), p. 261.

32. Tourgée, "The South as a Field for Fiction," *The Forum*, VI (December, 1888), 409.

33. Tourgée is careful to point out the antagonistic attitude Southerners had toward men like Arthur Lovett who insisted on granting the Negro freedom. The distinction between the poor white and the Negro is underlined when Tourgée describes the community's opinion of Lovett's amours: "If a gentleman choose to amuse himself *as* a gentleman, we've no right to interfere," says one Southerner. "We've come to break up Mr. Lovett's disgraceful connection with a free-nigger, but if he's cast her off and took up with Betty Certain we've nothing to say, except to congratulate him on the improvement of his taste, beg his pardon for our untimely visit and wish him good evening" (Tourgée, *A Royal Gentleman*, p. 179).

34. McIlwaine, p. xxiv.

35. *Ibid.*, p. 242.

Chapter Three

1. Dibble, p. 50.

2. *Journal of the Constitutional Convention of the State of North Carolina Held in 1875* (Raleigh, 1875), pp. 131, 140, 187, 259, 264.

3. Tourgée had proposed "that no convict whose labor may be farmed out shall be punished for any failure of duty as a laborer except by a responsible officer of the State" (*Ibid.*, p. 259).

4. Tourgée had proposed an amendment to Article 10, Section 6

of the Constitution, which stated "that any act of illicit sexual intercourse between a white person and a negro, or a person of negro blood to the third degree, shall be a misdemeanor." (*Ibid.*, p. 264.)

5. *Ibid.*, pp. 74, 90.

6. Hamilton, pp. 640-41. This incident is reported in the *Raleigh Daily Sentinel,* Turner's paper, July 21, 1875. On the same date *The Greensboro Patriot*, another anti-Republican paper, reported that Tourgée attempted at various times to disrupt the convention: "After the members present had affixed their signature to the new Constitution on Monday night, Tourgée moved to take a recess for a quarter of an hour, flourishing, at the same time in his hand, a Freedman's Bureau song book.

"The motion being put was carried, and Tourgée then repaired to the Secretary's desk and struck up the song, 'We'll rally around the flag, boys.' This led to a Bedlam Scene."

7. Tourgée to his wife, September 23, 1875.

8. During the Presidential campaign of 1872, Tourgée had delivered numerous speeches in favor of Grant's re-election. These speeches were not only made in North Carolina but in New York as well. In a typical speech, delivered in Rochester, he praised Grant as a political leader who "had saved us from a terrible doom. No man but he could have broken up the fiendish Ku Klux."

9. Tourgée to Dr. Sutherland, April 15, 1877.

10. Tourgée, "In Memory of the Republican Party," The "C" Letters, as published in *The North State* (Greensboro, 1878), p. 24.

11. Tourgée, "The South as a Field for Fiction," p. 413.

12. Thomas Nelson Page, for example, wrote insignificant fiction when he used the North as a setting in *Gordon Keith* (1903) and *John Marvel, Assistant* (1909).

13. Dibble, p. 71. The obvious autobiographical element in the book contradicts the notion, held by many reviewers of the time, that the prototype of Markham Churr was James A. Garfield.

14. Tourgée, *Figs and Thistles* (New York, 1879), p. 350.

15. *Ibid.*, p. 425.

16. *Ibid.*, p. 475.

17. Tourgée, "A Study in Civilization," *The North American Review*, CXLIII (September, 1886), 253.

18. Wilson, p. 536.

Chapter Four

1. Joel Chandler Harris, *Gabriel Tolliver; a story of Reconstruction* (New York, 1902), p. 291.

2. This anecdote is reported by Mildred Lewis Rutherford, *The*

South in History and Literature, A Handbook of Southern Authors (Atlanta, Georgia, 1906), p. 607.

3. Tourgée, *A Fool's Errand* (New York, 1879), p. 4.

4. *Ibid.*, p. 4.

5. Paul H. Buck, *The Road to Reunion, 1865-1900* (Boston, 1937), p. 68.

6. Tourgée, *A Fool's Errand*, p. 3.

7. *Ibid.*, p. 20.

8. *Ibid.*, p. 22.

9. It must be emphasized, once again, that nowhere in *A Fool's Errand* does Tourgée intimate that he and other Radical Republicans were at least partially responsible for the South's resistance to Northern ideas.

10. Tourgée, *A Fool's Errand*, p. 42.

11. *Ibid.*, p. 46.

12. H. L. Swint, *The Northern Teacher in the South 1862-1870* (Nashville, 1941), p. 163.

13. *American Freedman*, I (November, 1886), 114.

14. Swint, pp. 28, 141.

15. Tourgée, *A Fool's Errand*, p. 43.

16. *Ibid.*, p. 49.

17. *Ibid.*, p. 50.

18. *Ibid.*, p. 56.

19. *Ibid.*, p. 73.

20. *Ibid.*, pp. 129-30.

21. *Ibid.*, p. 111.

22. Walter Lynwood Fleming, *The Sequel of Appomattox, a Chronicle of the Reunion of the States* (New Haven, 1919), pp. 117-78.

23. *Ritual, Constitution and By-Laws of the National Council, Union League of America, Together with all Necessary Information for the Complete Working of Subordinate Council* (Washington, 1867).

24. Fleming, p. 191.

25. Tourgée to E. H. Johnson, May 15, 1902. Johnson was reviewing Thomas Dixon's *The Leopard's Spots*, a book that attacked the Union League and Radical Republicanism, and in this same letter asked Tourgée's opinion of the novel. "Entirely worthless as a narration of events or an analysis of events," answered Tourgée.

26. Donald, p. 10. See also Cortez A. M. Ewing, "Two Reconstruction Impeachments," *The North Carolina Historical Review*, XV (July, 1938), 206.

27. Horn, p. 31.

28. Tourgée, *A Fool's Errand*, p. 140.

29. *Ibid.*, p. 141.

30. *Ibid.*, p. 142.

31. *Ibid.*, p. 82.

32. Horn, p. 190.

33. *Ibid.*, p. 29. Founded in Pulaski, Tennessee, in 1865, the Klan's original purpose was purely social, and the young desperadoes were only in search of fun and mischief, frightening the highly superstitious Negroes. But as members discovered their influence on the colored man, they began "to act as a sort of police patrol and to hold in check thieving negroes, the Union League, and the 'loyalists.' " Soon an elaborate organization was formed, with a leader called the Grand Wizard, and sub-leaders of descending importance called Genii, Grand Dragons, Hydras, Grand Titans, Furies, Grand Giants, Goblins, Grand Cyclops, and Nighthawks. The general objectives of the order were set forth in a Prescript: "first, to protect the weak, the innocent, and the defenceless from the indignities, wrongs and outrages of the lawless, the violent, and the brutal; to relieve the injured and oppressed; to succor the suffering and unfortunate, and especially the widows and orphans of Confederate soldiers; second, to protect the States and people thereof from all invasion from any source whatever; third, to aid and assist in the execution of all 'constitutional' laws, and to protect the people from unlawful arrest, and from trial except by their peers according to the law of the land." *Ibid.*, p. 38. For a complete analysis of the growth of the Ku Klux Klan, the realms in various states, and the final decline of the Empire, see Horn, *Invisible Empire*.

34. Tourgée, *A Fool's Errand*, p. 169.

35. *Ibid.*, p. 171.

36. Wilson, p. 535.

37. Tourgée, *A Fool's Errand*, p. 190.

38. *Ibid.*, p. 192.

39. *Ibid.*, pp. 193-94.

40. Though many contemporary critics compared Uncle Jerry with Uncle Tom in Harriet Beecher Stowe's *Uncle Tom's Cabin*, the debt is only physical. Uncle Tom, a total pacifist, bears little resemblance to the vitriolic Uncle Jerry. Uncle Jerry is based on Wyatt Outlaw, the Negro president of the Union League who was hanged by the Ku Klux Klan on February 26, 1870, near the courthouse in Raleigh. Tourgée's description of Uncle Jerry's hanging resembles in almost every detail that of Outlaw. See *Holden Trial*, II, 363-69 and *Senate Report*, pp. 18, 259-60, 265-67.

41. Tourgée, *A Fool's Errand*, pp. 205-6.

42. *Ibid.*, p. 206.

43. *Ibid.*, p. 208.

44. See Horn, p. 194, for further corroboration on this point. Also, at the Testimonials of the Conditions of Affairs in the Southern

States, many former Ku Klux Klan members admitted that influential citizens led the Klan in its early stages. Jacob A. Long, the first Commander in Graham, Alamance County, listed a number of former members and agreed that they were all men of position and influence in the county. *Senate Report*, p. 261.

45. New York *Tribune*, April 4, 1881, p. 5.

46. Thomas Dixon, *The Leopard's Spots, A Romance of the White Man's Burden* (New York, 1902), p. 150.

47. Page, *Red Rock*, p. 351.

48. *Ibid.*, p. 528.

49. Harris, *Gabriel Tolliver*, p. 259.

50. Dixon, *The Leopard's Spots*, p. 150.

51. Wilson, p. 535.

52. Frank Nash, "Albion Winegar Tourgée," *Biographical History of North Carolina*, ed. Samuel A. Ashe, IV, 447.

53. Tourgée to R. M. Tuttle, May 26, 1870.

54. Tourgée, *A Fool's Errand*, p. 210.

55. Horn, p. 201. Tourgée's corrected letter appears in the New York *Tribune*, August 3, 1870, p. 2. The seriousness of Tourgée's statement should be emphasized, for many liberal Southerners who lived in and near Guilford County detested Tourgée for his false characterization of their homeland. As one resident of Guilford said, Tourgée "had never been able to verify that statement. He wrote the letter, and it got into the New York Tribune. I regarded it as exceedingly mendacious; as exaggerating in a very high degree, the state of crime in his circuit, and as bearing on its face the clear manifest purpose of merely agitating for political effect" (*Senate Report*, pp. 406-7).

56. Tourgée to J. C. Abbott, September 5, 1870.

57. Cortez A. M. Ewing, "Two Reconstruction Impeachments," *The North Carolina Historical Review*, XV (July, 1938), 209.

58. *Ibid.*, p. 208.

59. Holden's efforts to publicize the activities of the Klan did not accomplish his purpose, for the Republicans lost the state elections in 1870, and on January 23, 1871, Holden himself was impeached. The impeachment proceedings lasted until March 22, 1871, at which time the Democrats were successful in ousting Holden. During Holden's trial, some references were made to Tourgée as a judge. but he was never characterized as unfair or corrupt. See *Trial William W. Holden*, I, 536-65, 765-66, 777-78. For a fair account of Holden's impeachment see Cortez A. M. Ewing, "Two Reconstruction Impeachments," *The North Carolina Historical Review*, XV (July, 1938), 302-25.

60. Tourgée to Ralph Gorrell, C. P. Mendenhall, L. M. Scott, August 16, 1870.

61. Tourgée to Holden, May 17, 1870.
62. *Raleigh Daily Sentinel,* March 27, 1870.
63. Tourgée to Holden, undated letter.
64. Tourgée, *A Fool's Errand,* pp. 216-17.
65. *Ibid.,* p. 218.
66. *Ibid.,* p. 220.
67. See Nash, p. 447, for the actual incident upon which this adventure is based.
68. Tourgée, *A Fool's Errand,* p. 282.
69. *Ibid.,* p. 285.
70. *Ibid.,* p. 341.
71. *Ibid.,* p. 317.
72. *Ibid.,* p. 334.
73. *Ibid.,* pp. 358-59.
74. "Cynicus," *The Times Democrat,* June 18, 1905.
75. Devin, "Footprints of a Carpetbagger," p. 21.
76. Wilson, p. 545.
77. Tourgée, *A Fool's Errand,* pp. 346-47.
78. *The Union Register,* January 3, 1867.
79. Wilson, p. 537.
80. *The New York Tribune,* December 3, 1879, p. 6.
81. Quoted in Dibble, p. 68.
82. Quoted in Hope Chamberlain, *Old Days in Chapel Hill, Being the Life and Letters of Cornelia Phillips Spencer* (Chapel Hill, 1926), p. 190.
83. *Harper's Magazine,* LX (February, 1880), 472.
84. Smith, p. 63.
85. Tourgée, *Our Continent,* V (May 12, 1884), 604.
86. Dibble, p. 69.
87. William L. Royall, *A Reply to A Fool's Errand by One of the Fools* (New York, 1881), p. 3. Royall was a Southerner by birth, had fought for the confederacy, and then studied law in Richmond before joining the New York Bar.
88. Quoted in Dibble, p. 81.
89. N. J. Floyd, *Thorns in the Flesh* (New York, 1884), p. 5.
90. *Ibid.,* pp. 5-6.
91. *Ibid.,* p. 376.
92. *Ibid.,* p. 20.
93. *The Advance* (Lynchburg, Virginia), clipping in the Tourgée papers.

Chapter Five

1. Tourgée, *Bricks Without Straw* (New York, 1880), p. 111.
2. Tourgée, "The South as a Field for Fiction," p. 405.
3. *Ibid.,* p. 409.

4. Harris, *Gabriel Tolliver*, pp. 258-59.

5. *Ibid.*, pp. 162-63.

6. Page, "Marse Chan," *In Ole Virginia, or Marse Chan and other Stories* (New York, 1892), p. 10.

7. *The Nation*, XLV (September 22, 1881), 236.

8. Page, *The Old South, Essays Social and Political* (New York, 1911), pp. 314, 315. It is from this passage that Thomas Dixon derived the title of his novel, *The Leopard's Spots.*

9. Logan, p. 82.

10. Page, *The Red Riders* (New York, 1924), p. 91.

11. Sterling Brown, "The American Race Problem as Reflected in American Literature," *Journal of Negro Education*, VIII (July, 1929), 282.

12. Thomas Nelson Page to Arthur Hobson Quinn, n/d. Quoted in Arthur Hobson Quinn, *American Fiction, An Historical and Critical Survey* (New York, 1936), p. 360.

13. Northern authors imitated the Southern description of the Negro. See, as typical examples, Frank Stockton's *What Might Have Been Expected* (1874), *The Last Mrs. Null* (1886), and *The Christmas Wreck and Other Stories* (1886); Harriet Spofford's "A Thanksgiving Breakfast" in *Old Washington* (1906); and Constance Fenimore Woolson's "King David" in *Rodman the Keeper* (1886).

14. The image of the contented slave and the beneficent master was reinforced in almost all the fiction of the period. In Richard Meade Bache's *Under Palmetto* (1880), for example, the slave quarters are described as attractively as those of *Swallow Barn*; in Elizabeth Meriwether's *Black and White* (1883) a young white master studies at a medical college so that he can provide for the health of his servants.

For a realistic picture of the Southerner's attitude toward the Negro before and after the war, see William Gilmore Simms, *The Letters of William Gilmore Simms*, coll. and ed. Mary C. Simms Oliphant, Alfred Taylor Odell, and T. C. Eaves, I (Charleston, 1955), 343, 383, 502, 528. Before the war Simms could write to a friend, James Lawson, on March 17, 1861, that "I feed, physic, clothe, nurse & watch some 70 [Negroes], and have to live from hand to mouth myself—the mere steward of my negroes" (p. 353). Later in that same year, on November 18, he urged another friend, James Henry Hammond, to teach all Negroes "to feel that their owners are their best friends" (p. 383). But after the war, when the Negro was of little economic value to him, Simms discarded his paternal attitude; he knew now, as he wrote Evert A. Duyckinck on June 15, 1865, that he could "derive nothing from their labour, & what they shall make is yielded to them wholly" (p. 502). Soon he became openly bitter to the freedmen, and on December 19, 1865, wrote to Duyckinck that "the Negroes have been taught to believe that the lands of the country are to be divided among them, and they are no longer willing to work on any contract" (p. 528).

15. C. Vann Woodward, *Origins of the New South 1877-1913* (Baton Rouge, 1951), pp. 352, 356.

16. Dixon, *The Leopard's Spots*, p. 136.

17. *Ibid.*, pp. 150-51.

18. *Ibid.*, p. 196.

19. Thomas Dixon, *The Clansman*, p. 374. This novel was made into the film classic, *The Birth of the Nation. The Leopard's Spots* was converted into a successful play in 1903.

20. In the 1920's, when the Klan became active again, Dixon "repeatedly denounced the revived Ku Klux Klan as bigoted and in no way resembling its predecessor"; nevertheless "he regarded whites as 'superior' to Negroes." Quoted in obituary of Dixon, *The New York Times*, April 4, 1946.

21. See Dixon's report of the enormous success that a dramatization of *The Clansman* enjoyed in Charleston, South Carolina on October 25, 1905. Thomas Dixon, Jr., "Why I Wrote 'The Clansman'," *The Theatre*, VI (January, 1906), 20-22. In this article Dixon defends himself: "The accusation that I wrote 'The Clansman' to appeal to prejudice or assault the negro race is, of course, the silliest nonsense. For the negro I have only the profoundest pity and the kindliest sympathy" (p. 22). Dixon goes on to say that the Negro cannot live with the white man as an equal and that he should be colonized.

22. Tourgée to E. H. Johnson, May 15, 1902. See also a scathing attack on Dixon by a Negro, Kelly Miller, *As to The Leopard's Spots, An Open Letter to Thomas Dixon, Jr.* (Washington, 1905).

Dixon, born in 1864, had been ordained as a Baptist minister in 1887 at Raleigh, North Carolina, and preached in Raleigh, Boston, and New York; "his sermons were sensational" in nature. After having lived in New York for ten years, he resigned his pastorate and began to lecture. In 1901 he began his literary career, writing *A Leopard's Spots*. He died on April 3, 1946. Mildred Lewis Rutherford, *The South in History and Literature* (Atlanta, 1906), pp. 604-11.

23. Donald, p. 10.

24. Tourgée, "The South as a Field for Fiction," pp. 408, 409, 410.

25. Tourgée, *Bricks Without Straw*, p. 272.

26. *Ibid.*, p. 48.

27. Swint, p. 163.

28. *Ibid.*, p. 135. For further information in this regard, see A. D. Mayo, "Work of Certain Northern Churches in the Education of the Freedman, 1861-1900," *Report of the United States Commissioner of Education for 1901-1902* (Washington, 1902), pp. 285-314.

29. *The Dial*, I (October, 1880), 110-12.

30. Tourgée, *Bricks Without Straw*, pp. 158-59.

31. *Ibid.*, p. 256.

32. *Ibid.*, p. 307.

33. *Ibid.*, pp. 288-89.

34. *Ibid.*, p. 416.

35. *Ibid.*, p. 420.

36. *Ibid.*, p. 519.

37. In *Bricks Without Straw* he merely states this idea generally; it is in *An Appeal to Caesar* that Tourgée offers a thorough and detailed program of education. See pp. 114-16 for a full treatment of Tourgee's views on education.

38. Tourgée, *Bricks Without Straw*, p. 521.

Chapter Six

1. Tourgée, *John Eax and Mamelon, or The South Without the Shadow* (New York, 1882), p. 24.

2. *Ibid.*, p. 144.

3. *Ibid.*, p. 192.

4. Dibble, pp. 46-47.

5. Frank Luther Mott, *A History of American Magazines, III: 1865-1885* (Cambridge, 1938), 557.

6. Tourgée, *Our Continent*, III (March, 14, 1883), 345.

7. *Ibid.* The price of the magazine was ten cents a copy. He succeeded in pleasing the popular taste at the outset, for "in three days after the first issue was out, 58,000 copies of it had been sold." But the popularity soon waned, and Tourgée realized that $4.00 yearly subscriptions were not going to pour in. By the early part of 1884 circulation dropped to 4,000 (Mott, III, 558).

8. Tourgée, *Our Continent*, V (May 31, 1882), 249.

9. See *ibid.*, II (November 8, 1882), 571.

10. See *ibid.*, II (June 20, 1883), 794, for a typical statement.

11. Quoted in Dibble, p. 90.

12. Tourgée, *Hot Plowshares* (New York, 1883), p. iv.

13. Tourgée, *Our Continent*, I (June 21, 1882), 290.

14. Tourgée, *Hot Plowshares*, p. 145.

15. *Ibid.*, pp. iii-iv.

16. J. B. Ford to Tourgée, February 3, 1875.

17. George W. Cable, *The Negro Question*, ed. Arlin Turner (New York, 1958), p. xiii.

18. *Idem.*

19. Gunnar Myrdal, *An American Dilemma, The Negro Problem and Modern Democracy* (New York, 1944), p. 460.

20. Tourgée to E. H. Johnson, May 15, 1902.

21. Tourgée, "The Renaissance of Nationalism," *The North American Review*, CXLIV (January, 1887), *passim*.

22. Tourgée, "Shall White Minorities Rule?" *The Forum*, VII (April, 1889), 151.

23. Tourgée, *An Appeal to Caesar* (New York, 1884). This volume fulfilled a promise to President Garfield (although it appeared too late for Garfield to make use of Tourgée's idea). Garfield, who was a childhood friend of Tourgée, had read and enjoyed *A Fool's Errand*, and knew the book would aid his campaign of 1880. He asked Tourgée to assist him, and the latter enthusiastically made campaign speeches throughout the country for the Republican candidate. In June of 1881, after being elected, Garfield asked Tourgée to come to Washington for a conference regarding educational methods. After a two hours' meeting, Garfield said: "You are right. There is no other way. We must begin—*at the beginning*. Write out your views of what is possible to be done and let me have them—or, better still, put them into a book and I will study it. Of course I must find my own way in this matter, but you can help me. No one else has studied the subject in the same way or from the same standpoint that you have occupied. . . . You must help me in this matter." Tourgée, *An Appeal to Caesar*, p. 17.

Tourgée hopes to persuade the Republican party (the "Caesar" in the title) to legislate his life-long goal—national aid to education. The book contains statistics indicating the high rate of illiteracy in the South and details the need for national education and Tourgée's proposed remedy.

24. Tourgée, *An Appeal to Caesar*, p. 315.

25. *Ibid.*, p. 324.

26. *Ibid.*, pp. 332-33.

27. *Ibid.*, p. 319.

28. *Ibid.*, p. 337.

29. *Ibid.*, p. 332.

30. *Ibid.*, p. 169.

31. Rayford W. Logan, *The Negro in American Life and Thought, The Nadir 1877-1901* (New York, 1954), p. 82.

32. *Ibid.*, p. 83.

33. Tourgée, "A Man of Destiny," *Inter Ocean*, December 13, 1884, p. 13.

34. *Ibid.*, December 20, 1884, p. 13; December 27, 1884, p. 13; April 28, 1894, p. 13.

35. *Ibid.*, December 20, 1884, p. 12.

36. *Ibid.*, March 19, 1886, p. 4.

37. *Ibid.*, March 27, 1886, p. 12.

38. *Ibid.*, March 20, 1886, p. 13.

39. Some political comments in the 1890's are partisan to the point of absurdity. In 1892 he stated that "unless different governmental methods were used, there would be an uprising of the Negroes within the next ten years that would equal if not exceed the French Revolution in terror and bloodshed. Both the Northern and Southern press joined in vigorous condemnation of this new Tourgée jeremiad, but he insisted that the new prophecy would come true and used the columns of the *Inter Ocean* for defending himself in his usual intrepid fashion. As late as 1903, in a letter to Nixon [the editor of the *Inter Ocean*], he still maintained that such an uprising, accompanied with terrible slaughter, was almost inevitable" (Dibble, p. 116).

Chapter Seven

1. Tourgée, "Migma," *Our Continent*, IV (September 26, 1883), 411.

2. Tourgée, "The South as a Field for Fiction," p. 411.

3. Tourgée, "Migma," *Our Continent*, IV (September 26, 1883), 411.

4. There are notable exceptions to this generalization, among them Sarah Orne Jewett and Constance Fenimore Woolson.

5. Henry James, *The Selected Letters of Henry James,* ed. Leon Edel (New York, 1955), pp. 202-3. The date of this letter is October 5, 1901.

6. Harris, it should be remarked, was more tolerant of the early James than the later. See Julia Collier Harris, *The Life and Letters of Joel Chandler Harris* (Boston, 1918), p. 567; Jay B. Hubbell, *The South in American Literature* (Durham, 1954), p. 791.

7. Harris, *The Life of Joel Chandler Harris*, pp. 567-68.

8. Tourgée, "A Bystander's Notes," *Inter Ocean*, September 28, 1899, p. 4.

9. Tourgée, "Migma," *Our Continent*, III (June 6, 1883), 733.

10. Tourgée, "A Bystander's Notes," *Inter Ocean*, September 28, 1899, p. 4.

11. Tourgée, "Migma," *Our Continent*, II (December 27, 1882), 796-97. Harris was in complete agreement with Tourgée regarding Zola: "He disliked Zola and the French realists," his biographer notes, "never able to appreciate Zola's epic quality, because of the mass of sordid details that obscure the basic grandeur of his social ideal." Harris, *The Life of Joel Chandler Harris*, p. 586.

12. Tourgée, "A Bystander's Notes," *Inter Ocean*, September 28, 1899, p. 4.

13. Tourgée, "Migma," *Our Continent*, I (March 1, 1882), 40.

14. Tourgée, "Migma," *Our Continent*, III (April 18, 1883), 509.

15. Tourgée, "A True Fiction," *Our Continent*, IV (December 5, 1884), 731.

16. Tourgée, "Migma," *Our Continent*, III (January 6, 1883), 732.

17. Tourgée, *An Outing With the Queen of Hearts* (New York, 1894), pp. 55-56.

18. Tourgée, "Migma," *Our Continent*, III (June 6, 1883), 732.

19. Dibble, p. 102.

20. Tourgée, *Black Ice* (New York, 1887), p. 18.

21. Dibble, p. 103.

22. Tourgée, *Button's Inn* (Boston, 1887), p. 237.

23. *Ibid.*, p. 265.

24. Buck, p. 203.

25. Tourgée, *Letters to a King* (Cincinnati, 1888), p. 5.

26. *Ibid.*, p. 170.

27. *Ibid.*, p. 31.

28. Tourgée, *With Gauge and Swallow* (Philadelphia, 1889), pp. 5-6.

29. Dibble, p. 113.

30. Tourgée, *Murvale Eastman, Christian Socialist* (New York, 1889), p. 124.

31. *Ibid.*, p. 111.

32. *Ibid.*, p. 385.

33. *Ibid.*, p. 144.

34. *Ibid.*, p. 187.

35. *Ibid.*, p. 166.

36. *Ibid.*, p. 430.

37. *Ibid.*, p. 209.

38. *Ibid.*, p. 269.

39. Arthur Hobson Quinn, ed., *The Literature of the American People* (New York, 1951), p. 770.

40. Quoted by Tourgée, "A Bystander's Notes," *Daily Inter Ocean*, May 10, 1890, p. 4.

41. Tourgée, *Pactolus Prime* (New York, 1890), p. 130.

42. *Ibid.*, p. ii.

43. The actual plot of Pactolus Prime is the most preposterous of all Tourgée's novels. Prime, who is so dark he appears to be a pure-bred Negro, has a beautiful "white" daughter called Eva to whom he has been giving money (though she does not know who her benefactor is). Eva intuitively senses that she has Negro blood—despite the fact that her knowledge of her own past is obscure—and she feels a strange attraction to Prime, the bootblack. Pactolus is fatally injured and brought to Eva's home where a doctor proves that this bootblack is not colored at all; and Prime, after his death, leaves a statement of his life, clarifying his mysterious background.

Born of a slave mother and a white father, Pactolus (white in appearance) was "schooled" for fun by his master and later deprived of his fiancée, May, by that same master. Prime left to fight for the Union forces, and when he returned to the Southern plantation he discovered that May had been seduced by his master and had had a child by him. Prime married May and took her and her child (a boy, Benny) to the North, but on the highway he was shot by his old master. While recovering he discovered that his hair had fallen out and that his skin had become black.

As a colored man and bootblack, Pactolus Prime served senators and Washington legislators. Benny, the son of May and Prime's white master, became Pactolus' assistant. After his death, Prime's daughter enters a nunnery, having decided to devote her work to the colored people.

44. Tourgée, *Pactolus Prime*, p. 166.

45. *Ibid.*, p. 12.

46. *Ibid.*, p. 111.

47. Tourgée, "A Bystander's Notes," *Inter Ocean*, August 22, 1891, p. 4.

48. Buck, p. 306.

49. Fred Lewis Pattee, *A History of American Literature Since 1870* (New York, 1915), p. 318.

50. Tourgée, *The Man Who Outlived Himself* (New York, 1898), pp. 12-13.

51. *Ibid.*, p. 68.

52. Dibble, p. 93.

Chapter Eight

1. See "A Quiet Corner in Europe," *The Independent*, LI (June 1, 1899), 1483-85; "Our Consular System," *The Independent*, LIV (January 23, 1902), 208-10; and "Some Advice to Young Voters," *The Golden Rule* (October 1, 1896), pp. 4-5.

2. Logan, pp. 35, 37.

3. *Ibid.*, p. 151.

4. *Ibid.*, pp. 171, 178.

5. *Ibid.*, p. 216.

6. Dibble, p. 126.

7. Tourgée to E. H. Johnson, May 15, 1902.

8. Tourgée, "The South as a Field for Fiction," *The Forum*, VI (December, 1888), 405.

9. Tourgée to E. H. Johnson, May 15, 1902.

10. Wilson, p. 535.

11. Tourgée, "Migma," *Our Continent*, V (May 19, 1884), 635.

Selected Bibliography

PRIMARY SOURCES

Manuscripts

The Tourgée manuscripts are in the Chautauqua County Historical Museum, Westfield, Chautauqua County, New York. In addition to the drafts of short poems and essays, most of which were never published, the more important original manuscripts to be found at the museum are the following: "God's Anynted Phue" (essays written for *New-Berne Republican-Courier* in 1871); *Bricks Without Straw* (1880); *Zouri's Christmas* (a short novel, published with *A Royal Gentleman* in 1881); *John Eax* (1882); *A Man of Destiny* (articles written for the Chicago *Inter Ocean* in 1884 and 1885); *The Veteran and His Pipe* (essays published in the *Inter Ocean* in 1885); and *With Gauge and Swallow* (short stories about the legal profession, published in *Lippincott's Monthly Magazine* from 1887-89).

There are approximately fifteen hundred letters in the Tourgée collection. Nearly all of them were written by Tourgée while he lived in the South. As a politician and a circuit judge, Tourgée traveled a great deal, and he wrote to his wife almost every day. These letters —ranging in date from 1865, when Tourgée was looking for a home in North Carolina, until the 1877 state elections—are too personal to have much interest for anyone except the biographer. In them Tourgée almost never speaks of political issues; he is constantly concerned about his wife's health and about small domestic matters.

Of far more interest—and of indispensable value to anyone writing of Tourgée—are several books Tourgée kept while he was a judge; these books contain carbon copies of the letters he wrote between 1868 and 1874 and are primarily political in nature. Many letters, written by local friends, were sent to Tourgée during this period; and, when he left North Carolina in 1879, lawyers in the state wrote to him to express their admiration for his work as a judge. An illuminating letter—really a "document," for it is thirty-five pages in length and completely impersonal—was written by Tourgée in 1902 to E. H. Johnson, a critic who was reviewing Thomas Dixon's *The Leopard's Spots*; this letter contains the clearest statement of Tourgée's final views regarding the Negro and Reconstruction.

Equally as important as those letters concerned with political affairs in North Carolina are Tourgée's *Superior Court Record Books,* records of the cases over which he presided as a Superior Court judge; these records are helpful in determining Tourgée's role as a judge.

Tourgée kept several scrapbooks which contain reviews of his various novels—those criticizing *A Royal Gentleman* are the greatest in number—and many newspaper clippings which refer to him as a "corrupt judge" and an "unscrupulous politician." Together with this material are the more important obituaries written at the time of Tourgée's death, collected in a scrapbook by his wife and daughter.

Tourgée was an indefatigable speech-maker. In addition to many political addresses that he delivered when he lived in North Carolina, he also gave formal speeches before various groups of sympathetic listeners. The drafts of these speeches are in the collection at the Chatauqua County Historical Museum; some of their titles indicate their general subject matter: "The Ben Adhemite Era" (1875-1876), "Southern Humor" (1875-1876), "The Education of the Negro" (August 30, 1881), "The Elevation of the Negro" (1885), "Oration on Grant" (1885), "The Nation and the Negro" (April 15, 1888), "The Negro in America" (1889), and "On Union Soldiers" (1895). Little additional knowledge is gained from a perusal of these speeches; they are restatements of the ideas which appear in Tourgée's fiction and journalistic writings.

The collection in Westfield includes materials which have not been used in this study. There are youthful letters to Tourgée's parents, a school notebook containing only lecture notes for courses Tourgée took in his high school, a college essay on "Japan as a Missionary Field," albums of family photographs, and ledgers of the Handle Company he established in Greensboro. This material does not illuminate Tourgée's activities in the South but would, of course, be invaluable for the writing of a full-length biography. Roy F. Dibble makes use of most of this material in his biography, *Albion W. Tourgée* (1921), but he neglects the important papers dealing with Tourgée as a carpetbagger in North Carolina.

Books

An Appeal to Caesar. New York: Fords, Howard, and Hulbert, 1884.
Black Ice. New York: Fords, Howard, and Hulbert, 1888.
Bricks Without Straw. New York: Fords, Howard, and Hulbert, 1880.
Button's Inn. Boston: Roberts Brothers, 1887.
Eighty-Nine. Edited from the original manuscript, by Edgar Henry.
    New York: Cassell and Co., 1891.
Figs and Thistles: A Romance of the Western Reserve. New York:
    Fords, Howard, and Hulbert, 1879.
A Fool's Errand. New York: Fords, Howard, and Hulbert, 1879;

reprinted by John Hope Franklin, ed. Cambridge: Harvard University Press, 1961.

Hot Plowshares. New York: Fords, Howard, and Hulbert, 1883.

The Invisible Empire. New York: Fords, Howard, and Hulbert, 1879-80.

John Eax and Mamelon, Or The South Without A Shadow. New York: Fords, Howard, and Hulbert, 1882.

Letters To A King. Cincinnati: Cranstone & Stowe, 1888.

The Man Who Outlived Himself. New York: Fords, Howard, and Hulbert, 1898.

The Mortgage on the Hip-Roof House. Cincinnati: Jennings and Graham, 1896.

Murvale Eastman, Christian Socialist. New York: Fords, Howard, and Hulbert, 1889-90.

Out of the Sunset Sea. New York: Merill and Baker, 1893.

An Outing with the Queen of Hearts. New York: Merill and Baker, 1894.

Pactolus Prime. New York: Cassell and Co., 1890.

A Royal Gentleman and Zouri's Christmas. New York: Fords, Howard, and Hulbert, 1881.

A Son of Old Harry. New York: Robert Bonner's Sons, 1891 and 1892.

The Story of a Thousand, Being a History of the Service of the 105th Ohio Volunteer Infantry, in the War for the Union from August 21, 1862 to June 6, 1865. Buffalo: S. McGerald & Son, 1896.

The Veteran and His Pipe. Chicago: Belford, Clark & Co., 1888.

The War of the Standards. New York: Merill and Baker, 1896.

With Gauge and Swallow, Attorneys. Philadelphia: J. B. Lippincott, 1889.

Articles, Newspapers, and Periodicals

"Aaron's Rod in Politics," *The North American Review,* CXXXII (February, 1881), 139-62.

"The Anti-Trust Campaign," *The North American Review* (July, 1893), 30-40.

"An Astral Partner," *The Green Bag* (July-August, 1896).

The Basis. Weekly, March-December, 1895; monthly, December-April, 1896. Buffalo.

"A Bystander's Notes," *Inter Ocean,* May, 1888-January, 1895; August, 1897-September, 1898.

"A Child of Luck," *Inter Ocean,* March-July, 1886.

"The Christian Citizen," *The Chautauquan,* II (November, 1881), 86-91.

"John Workman's Notions," *Inter Ocean,* July, 1891-May, 1892.

"Letters To A Mugwump," *Inter Ocean,* September-November, 1885.

"A Man of Destiny," *Inter Ocean,* December, 1884-March, 1885; January-April, 1894.

"Our Consular System," *The Independent,* LIV (January 23, 1902), 208-10.

Our Continent, A Weekly Illustrated Magazine Conducted by Albion W. Tourgée. Philadelphia: Our Continent Publishing Co., February 15, 1882-August 20, 1884.

"A Quiet Corner in Europe," *The Independent,* LI (June 1, 1899), 1483-85.

"Reform versus Reformation," *The North American Review* (April, 1881), 305-19.

"The Renaissance of Nationalism," *The North American Review,* CXLIV (January, 1887), 1-11.

"The Reversal of Malthus," *The American Journal of Sociology,* II (July, 1896), 13-24.

"The Right to Vote," *The Forum,* VIII (March, 1890), 78-92.

"Shall White Minorities Rule?" *The Forum,* VII (April, 1889), 143-55.

"The South as a Field for Fiction," *The Forum,* VI (December, 1888), 404-13.

"A Study in Civilization," *The North American Review,* CXLIII (September, 1886), 246-61.

"The Summerdale Brabble," *The National Tribune,* March-April, 1901.

"The Twentieth Century Peacemakers," *Contemporary Review,* LXXV (June, 1899), 886-908.

The Union Register. Weekly, January 3-June 14, 1867. Greensboro.

Public Document

The Code of Civil Procedure of North Carolina, with notes and decisions by Albion W. Tourgée. Raleigh: J. Nichols, 1878.

SECONDARY SOURCES

Only those works directly related to Tourgée are listed. The vast amount of background material necessary for a complete understanding of Tourgée and Reconstruction is indicated in the footnotes. In general, if the critic relies on J. G. deRoulhac Hamilton, *Reconstruction in North Carolina* (New York, 1914) for his historical information and does not take into account the revised interpretation of Reconstruction by modern historians, his work will lack authority. Furthermore, little will be learned of Tourgée and Reconstruction unless the reader is given a rather full account, based on the unpublished material in the Tourgée collection, of Tourgée's life in North Carolina.

Books

DIBBLE, ROY F. *Albion W. Tourgée*. New York: Lemcke & Buechner, 1921. Only biography of Tourgée; valuable for a general outline of Tourgée's life. Dibble's information is accurate though very limited; he has little to say regarding Reconstruction or Tourgée's experiences in North Carolina. The criticism of Tourgée's fiction is marred by Dibble's hostile attitude toward his subject.

GROSS, THEODORE L. *Albion W. Tourgée: Reporter of the Reconstruction*. Unpublished Ph.D. dissertation, Columbia University, 1960. A study of Tourgée's role in Reconstruction and his fictional achievement. Tourgée is seen in context with other writers of Reconstruction.

OLSEN, OTTO HAROLD. *A Carpetbagger: Albion W. Tourgée and Reconstruction in North Carolina*. Unpublished Ph.D. dissertation, The Johns Hopkins University, 1959. A thorough account of Tourgée as a political figure in the Reconstruction period. Olsen offers a new and persuasive evaluation of Tourgée's role as a carpetbagger, seeing him as basically a humanitarian. He places Tourgée in historical perspective, offering a modern historical approach to Tourgée's diverse activities and to Reconstruction in North Carolina.

Essays

BECKER, GEORGE J. "Albion W. Tourgée: Pioneer in Social Criticism," *American Literature*, XIX (March, 1947), 59-72. This essay, a sensible though superficial introduction to Tourgée's important Reconstruction fiction, relies on Dibble's biographical information. Becker asks for a reappraisal of Tourgée's contribution to American literature.

COWIE, ALEXANDER. *The Rise of the American Novel*. New York: American Book Company, 1949. Favorable, generally accurate commentary on Tourgée's fiction.

DEVIN, WILLIAM A. Footprints of a Carpetbagger," *The Torch*, XVII (April, 1944), 16-19, 21. Defends Tourgée as an honest judge and as a carpetbagger with the best of intentions. He uses little evidence to support his claim.

NILON, CHARLES HAMPTON. *Some Aspects of the Treatment of Negro Characters by Five Representative American Novelists: Cooper, Melville, Tourgée, Glasgow, Faulkner*. Unpublished Ph.D. dissertation, University of Wisconsin, 1952. Treats Tourgée as one of five American novelists who have commented extensively on Negro problems. Some insights are perceptive, but in general they are limited because Nilon does not consider Tourgée's role in Reconstruction.

NYE, RUSSELL B. "Judge Tourgée and Reconstruction," *The Ohio State Archaeological Review*, XXI (July, 1941), 101-14. An historical essay which treats Reconstruction and Tourgée's role in North Carolina too simply. Nye, because he does not make use of the Tourgée papers, sees Tourgée as too typical a carpetbagger and Radical Republican.

WEISBLUM, TED N. "Albion W. Tourgée: Propagandist and Critic of Reconstruction," *The Ohio Historical Quarterly*, Vol. 70 (January, 1961), 26-44. Discusses *A Fool's Errand* and *Bricks Without Straw*. This essay, which characterizes Tourgée as a corrupt carpetbagger, is marred by historical information based exclusively on Hamilton's *Reconstruction in North Carolina*.

WILSON, EDMUND, "Novelists of the Post-War South: Albion W. Tourgée, George W. Cable, Kate Chopin, Thomas Nelson Page," *Patriotic Gore: Studies in the Literature of the American Civil War*. New York: Oxford University Press, 1962. Effective, sympathetic presentation of Tourgée. Wilson considers *A Fool's Errand* an "historical classic" and examines the book in some detail. Shows that Tourgée had an exceptional understanding of Reconstruction problems, a sympathy for the Southern point of view, and a wise solution to the difficulties of the Negro.

Index

Index

813.49
T645

73/50

DATE DUE